God & Therapy

*what we believe
when no one is watching*

iBooks
Habent Sua Fata Libelli

iBooks
Manhanset House
Shelter Island Hts., New York 11965-0342
Tel: 212-427-7139
bricktower@aol.com • www.ibooksinc.com

Library of Congress Cataloging-in-Publication Data

Alper, Gerald
God & Therapy, what we believe when no one is watching
p. cm.

1. Psychology—General 2. Psychology—Cognitive 3. Psychology—Clinical
4. Psychology—Psychotherapy 5. Theology—Philosophy
Non-Fiction, I. Title.

ISBN: 978-1-59687-435-0, Trade Paper

January 2016

God & Therapy

*what we believe
when no one is watching*

Gerald Alper

To the memory of

My Father

and of

My Mother

CONTENTS

PREFACE

It is often said that there are no atheists in foxholes. I don't
know if I believe that. I do believe that there are no skeptics
when it comes to believing in hope. That we always, in Daniel
Dennett's felicitous phrase, continue to "believe in belief." We
may feel we have reached the end of the tether. We may give
up, succumb to a growing despair, devoutly wish for escape,
sleep, peace, nirvana. But never do we wish for extinction, for
nothingness, for pure emptiness. Always we want something.
To wish at long last for an end to all suffering, fighting, hoping
is not to wish for nothing. It is to wish for something: so long
as there is life, hope never stops twitching.

This is a book about what people in their heart of hearts, when
no one is looking, believe or don't believe before organized
religion, political correctness, and group pressure gathers them
up in its collective grasp. It is a psychodynamic axiom that
death does not exist in the unconscious. If that is true, then
neither does the afterlife. Neither do angels, the pearly gates or
heaven. There is, however, in addition to hope and belief, a very
profound desire to be paid attention to, to be cared for, to be
reassured. There is a deep yearning for an oceanic connection to
a powerful, cosmic, parental figure to be called upon primarily
when the need is desperate. Such a cosmic, parental figure is
both masculine and feminine. Masculine when decisive action—
protection or vengeance—is what is required. Feminine when
we want—against all the dictates of reason—for the inexorable
cruelty of the laws of the cosmos to be suspended in our behalf

because a God-like being has just taken pity on us, because she loves us. This unconscious cosmic parent is neither omnipotent, omniscient nor omnibenevolent. It is not a cohesive, defined being. It is a transient being for the vast majority of people, that comes and goes, to be used selectively on a crisis-intervention basis.

This may be why in some ways, we—adults as well as children—are perhaps more afraid of the dark than of the afterlife. Close your eyes for a moment and see how easy it is to imagine that somewhere nearby a hidden presence threatens. I do not mean the rational fear that darkness is an invitation and refuge to the criminally minded. I am talking about the irrational fear that a perfectly secure room or house can in the flick of a light switch be converted into a haven for evil. Such a fear likely has Darwinian roots in our ancestral, hunter-gatherer past when our genome was taking final form. For while it may have been irrational to suspect every shadow, odd noise, or suspicious hush as signs of an interloper, if your neighbors are hyenas and carnivores, it can be adaptive (literally life-saving) to be an instinctive practitioner of a better-safe-than-sorry strategy.

Regarding religion, my position is that both faith and evidence-based belief can be true, but that they cannot be separated. To say you have faith without evidence, or belief without evidence, is equivalent to saying you have access to, can channel a different sense organ than the rest of us have. It is a claim not only made by the devout, but by professional psychics, those who boast they can read minds, perform feats of telekinesis and tune in regularly to the paranormal world. While that may be true, no one who is unwilling to submit their claims of special knowledge to a public test can legitimately proclaim to have proved it. The only type of valid knowledge about our shared world—which is what all religions profess to have—is knowledge that can be consensually validated. That means knowledge that can be invalidated, which means knowledge that can be submitted to and survive objective, public, critical scrutiny. You can't have it both ways.

That being said, and much as I admire Richard Dawkins and Sam Harris, I don't believe I could ever be as angry at the excesses of organized religion as they are. Nor could I be as certain of my core beliefs—the necessity, for example, for always maintaining an open, questioning frame of mind, to which I heartily subscribe—as they appear to be. And great as I think William James is, I would never want to walk that self-imposed tightrope he traversed for much of his life between rigorous, experimental psychology on the one hand and passionate, obsessive exploration of just about every conceivable paranormal phenomena on the other.

Today, there is an unprecedented worldwide effort by scientists to reframe and reconstitute religion as a natural phenomenon. As never before God and spirituality are being invited into the laboratory and the domain of evolutionary biology. An unending stream of new books are enthusiastically presenting their findings to the interested lay public. We have: *The God Delusion* by Richard Dawkins; *The God Gene* by Dean Hammer; *God: The Failed Hypothesis* by Victor Stenger; *Breaking the Spell* by Daniel Dennett; *The End of Faith* by Sam Harris; *The Varieties of Scientific Exploration: a Scientist's Personal View of the Search for God* by Carl Sagan; *Darwin for Everyone* by David Sloan Wilson (just published as I write this); and *Spook: Science investigates the afterlife* by Mary Roach. In these books, the relationship of the ordinary person to religion is studied from every imaginable angle. From the political, sociological, cultural, evolutionary, theological and neuroscientific viewpoint. But almost never from the therapeutic perspective.

So my own book began as a puzzle and a question. If, on the one hand, I believed, as nearly every therapist does, that the process of psychotherapy can offer a window on the deepest feelings people have on the crucial issues of their lives; and if it is true, as we are told over and over again, that the overwhelming majority of Americans believe in the existence of God, in heaven and in the intervention of angels, then, I had to ask myself,

> "Why, in over thirty years of private practice, after listening to hundreds and hundreds of patients' dreams, had I not once encountered the presence of God, the joyful fantasy of an afterlife, the radiant appearance of an angel? Why in the outpouring and welter of wishes, secrets and hopes to which a therapist regularly attends, was heaven never mentioned?"

While I am aware that America is teeming with millions of fundamentalists, to whom these beliefs are daily meat and drink, it is also true Jehovah's Witnesses, born-again, evangelical Christians, highly orthodox, Hasidic Jews and the like, do not come for therapy. They go to their pastor, their rabbi, or—in cases of ongoing crisis—to a pastoral counselor. In spite of that, I had an unusually broad data base to draw upon. In the course of three decades of private practice in New York City, I had engaged the full spectrum of mental and emotional duress. Prior to that, for nearly ten years, while pursuing a Fellowship at the American Institute for

Psychotherapy and Psychoanalysis, I had conducted literally thousands and thousands of clinical intake interviews of patients seeking psychological treatment. Upon graduating, I had proceeded to publish fifteen books and numerous papers in professional journals, covering many of the major dimensions of psychotherapy with the patients I had treated. Yet, when I reviewed all of my notes, I could find no mention of any supernatural agencies that could properly be called intrinsically religious. Some of my patients, on occasion, had brushes with what they thought were ghosts. Some heard voices. Many had dreams in which dead loved ones appeared as though alive and never having died. Some had spooky encounters with fortune tellers who often would astonish them with what they seemed to know, but could not have known. Some experienced utterly inexplicable, uncanny coincidences. Some were believers in astrology, or flattered themselves that they possessed genuine psychic powers. But no one had ever been visited by an angel; had a vision of the afterlife; or heard the voice of God. All of my patients were afraid of death, of the process of dying in particular, but none of them expressed undue concern over the fate of their soul in the immediate afterlife. No patient expressed what I would call genuine fear they might literally go to hell. None of them expressed a discernible desire to enter heaven. And this, I believed, was not the manifestation of urban cynicism and secular thinking. Not a single patient ever identified himself or herself as an atheist or even an agnostic. Almost all of them, in regard to the question of the existence of the afterlife, professed to believe in at least "something." And finally, of the thousands of patients I either interviewed or treated, I never encountered a single person who offered as their presenting problem the conflict over whether intelligent life arose accidentally or according to a divine intervention.

Gradually it dawned on me that between what people believed in the core of their being and what they were taught in Sunday School, Bible class, in the long course of their religious indoctrination—was a yawning gap. A gap that was hardly reflected in the answers given to pollsters, in the statistics of social scientists, in the brain studies of neuroscientists, and in the ever burgeoning speculative theories of evolutionary biologists. Why, I wondered, had the dreams, the reveries, secret wishes, free associations—that window into the inner self that only psychodynamic psychotherapy can provide—been so studiously bypassed?

So far as I know, my book is a first attempt to survey and sketch what might be called, for want of a better name, *the theology of the unconscious.* This is, of course, a bottom-up perspective and the reader should not be surprised that the picture it reveals is characterized by incoherence, inconsistency, self-contradiction, transience and instability. It is, in short, a typical product of the unconscious that scarcely resembles the canons and protocols of organized religion. After all, if the greatest of scientists such as Steven Weinberg can be candidly baffled as to how our universe originated, we cannot expect the average person to be impressively clear.

That said, it cannot be denied that there is a deep need in the average person that cannot be satisfied with either the so-called poetry of science or the quasi-religious, majestic awesomeness of our cosmos. There is a palpable yearning for a genuine transcendental 'something,' a spiritual other that, somehow, albeit incomprehensibly, is capable of joining us in a personal, emotional and anthropomorphic connectedness. If this is true, that there is no question more important to us than whether there is a transpersonal, spiritual basis to our existence, then it is also true that—unless we are one of those rare souls who can blissfully surrender our minds and hearts to the conversion experience—we must resign ourselves that we will never come close to an unassailable answer in our lifetimes.

We immediately see our dilemma. No question is more urgent than whether the cosmos is indifferent to our pain and suffering and no question is more unanswerable.

We are left with the daunting prospect of learning to live with a haunting uncertainty, with always resisting the tempting consolations of easy certitude, always prepared, when reason demands it, to relinquish even our most cherished beliefs.

But if psychotherapy teaches us anything, it teaches us that when it comes to religious beliefs, the child is father to the man. People are remarkably unwilling, uninterested and unmotivated to be creative or critically daring when it comes to choosing their personal theology. In each of us, there is a residue of childish hunger for cosmic protection and connectedness that we never entirely surmount. For this residue—critical questions concerning the ultimate meaning of our place in the cosmos—are no more relevant than the ancient paradoxes of Zeno are to the person who is dancing. And there's the rub. If belief in the afterlife is a primitive, deeply emotional and somehow necessary statement about our place in the universe, then it is likely to be profoundly resistant to the kind of cool, skeptical thinking that is a signature of the modern mind.

Nevertheless, no law of the universe says we are doomed to succumb to our childish past when it comes to our philosophy of religion. Even the most ironclad of theological dogmas—that our fate in the afterlife is literally to spend an eternity in either heaven or hell—allows for radical choice, the ability of each person, in the final accounting, to determine their ultimate destiny. In other words, even if the choices of good and evil are strictly provided by a judgmental God, what we ultimately make of those choices rests solely in our hands. And psychotherapy shows that, regardless of religious beliefs, the overwhelming majority of people live their lives with a dubious relationship at best with the transcendental being of their choice. It is only when we are faced with—or forced to contemplate the prospect of—life being taken away, snuffed out, that the issue of whether the cosmos literally cares for us, has a plan for us, becomes paramount.

Ironically, in this case, the question is more important than the answer. Although it may pose the ultimate paradox, nothing seems more important than how honestly, openly, passionately and wholeheartedly we embrace this question in our lives. If there is an answer—and we are lucky enough to find it—it will come after we die.

CHAPTER ONE

IF HEAVEN EXISTS . . .

Like clockwork, at the end of every televised presentation of Actor's Studio, the dour, professorial director, James Lipton, will ask his distinguished guest of the week a question that is always the same: "If Heaven exists, what would you like to hear God say to you?" Invariably the famous actor who has graciously consented to be interviewed before a room full of adoring students will reflectively pause, pretending to be hearing the question for the first time. At precisely the right moment, he or she will offer their answer, ranging typically from the meant-to-be-cute to the outright ridiculous . . . "Your room is just down the corridor," . . . "Bravo!"

Although clearly not meant to be a set up for comic relief, the question is hardly an invitation to existential soul-searching. Both question and answer reflect the peculiar no-man's land that people so readily fall into when queried about their religious faith. Rarely had this been more apparent than on the celebrated Barbara Walters' prime time ABC special, "Heaven—Where Is It? How do we get there?" (Dec. 2005). Presented as an investigative reporter's honest attempt to survey the thoughts and beliefs of people from all walks of life vis-à-vis heaven, we heard: balding Cardinal Theodore McCarrick, the Roman Catholic archbishop of Washington, hoping he would get his hair back in heaven; Jackie Mason saying in the hereafter he expected to eat pastrami without gaining weight;

an imam solemnly proclaiming that in the Muslim heaven, "we will be in comfortable homes, reclining on silk couches . . . beyond which rivers flow"; ordinary people claiming to have actually crossed over or seen the Light on operating tables or deathbeds, yet lived to tell about it; a woman who, while flatlining after complications from childbirth, said, "she found herself mounting a staircase toward an azure sky . . ."

Such are the dreams and fantasies of the afterlife. They are not so different from the hopes for a better life, a less pain-ridden, a kinder and gentler existence than that which they have known, to which a therapist daily listens. Except here they have been sanitized, sublimated and transported to another world. It is no accident that people's fantasies of the afterlife tend to stop short at the pearly gates. It does not seem to occur to James Lipton that perhaps the most realistic, the best answer to his question, "What would you like to hear God say to you?" might be "Nothing." That it would simply be too terrifying for the average person to endure the sickening suspense of waiting to discover the irrevocable fate lying in store for their immortal soul. That they might infinitely prefer to somehow already know—through some instantaneous angelic epiphany—that they have just, in the words of Charles Dickens' Sidney Carton, gone to "a far, far better place than I have ever gone to."

It takes only a moment's thought to realize that what people are interested in when it comes to the afterlife are not the details. It is the big picture that preoccupies them. Will there be something to look forward to? A presence, a feeling of love, a oneness? Or are they going to be judged and perhaps punished by a supernatural being? Will they be safe?

Although such questions are unanswerable, it is remarkable that they are almost never asked. In a famous philosophical essay, Thomas Nagel once wondered, "What is it like to be a bat?" He had come to believe that there are limits to human cognition; that, for example, no matter how much we learn about their neurophysiology we can never enter the experiential world of the bat and know what it is like to be a bat. Analogously, I think the same intrinsic limits exist when it comes to our capacity to empathize with the thoughts and feelings of a personal God. No matter how much religious training we have received, we cannot imagine what it would be like to relate in depth to an omniscient, omnipotent, infinitely benevolent being. We cannot conceive what it would be like to encounter in person and in depth a being who for the duration of our lives had been faceless, voiceless and tantalizingly hidden.

I am aware that numerous people have claimed, and may well have experienced, oceanic feelings, true conversions, religious ecstasies. Today, so-called altered realities are no longer restricted to the ingestion of a handful of esoteric hallucinogens. We have nightmares, hallucinations, out of body experiences, near death experiences, paranormal experiences. Each of us, as William James once said, has a world unto himself or herself. There is my world, yours, there's the world of dogs, cats, of bats, of every creature on earth. But these are all (from our perspective) *humanly or biologically altered worlds*. To attempt to emotionally relate in earnest to an infinite supernatural presence is something quite different. It is unimaginable. Unless, as Wittgenstein once said, we acquired a new sense. That would be equivalent, as mentioned, to saying you have a direct, mystical pipeline to another world. It, of course, is what the most devout religious people regularly claim. Unless you have been a believer from childhood on, or have experienced a life-altering conversion, it is the most unpersuasive of arguments. Perhaps the best answer to that is the fact that throughout history many if not most of the mystical experiences that have been duly recorded have contradicted one another.

To drive the point home, I would like to offer a thought experiment. A thought experiment is not something that could actually happen (although it might). It is something that is at least logically possible, something that does not violate in any flagrant way the laws of the universe. Its purpose is to dramatize in a single, psychological way, the enormous difficulty we all have when it comes to seriously and realistically envisioning the possibilities of an actual afterlife. To have any chance of doing that, it helps to stop short of the pearly gates. No one, not even the greatest of theologians, has dared to venture much further than that when it comes to imagining what it is like to encounter the presence of God. What can be imagined, however, and what many people have imagined, is the possibility that consciousness, or the self, or the soul, continues to exist in some form after the body dies.

In *Spook: Science tackles the afterlife*, Mary Roach offers a lively journalistic account of the current worldwide effort to do just that. Not surprisingly, by the book's end she reports the results could not be more inconclusive. At present, there is absolutely no proof either way. We are free to choose.

So let us imagine, for just a moment, the possibility that consciousness somehow does survive the death of the body. We cannot know the form or substance or mechanism by which such consciousness continues to live, but suppose (as we all would wish) that it is more or less intact, recognizably human and sensate. In *The First Three Minutes* Steven Weinberg wrote one of the grand books of scientific theorizing, a state-of-the-art, cutting-edge cosmological account of what happened right after the Big Bang. In our case, there is no science whatsoever to guide us. There is, however, for want of a better word, psychological plausibility, phenomenological verity. We have only to imagine, supposing that is, our consciousness has survived . . . in some inchoate form . . . in some limbo space . . . our death, and we might have . . .

The First Three Minutes of the Afterlife

You have just woken up, so the operation must be over. Your impulse is to call for the nurse, but something stops you. Whatever this place is you're in, it's not the recovery room. It may not even be the hospital. But you do remember, the last thing you remember, is your doctor giving you an injection with a sedative in it. Even though your chances of survival were over ninety percent, he looked worried. For a long time your heartbeat had been irregular, some kind of arrhythmia that could never be adequately accounted for. There would be pain afterwards, the doctor said, but there isn't pain, there isn't much of anything. You feel very strange, very different, you can't say how. Not sleepy, not really awake, your thoughts are coming in slow motion. Why can't you see anything, not even the shape of your hands in front of your face? It's not dark, not light, just kind of vaporous.

Suddenly getting nervous, you call out your own name, just to hear a familiar sound, to reassure yourself you are the same person waking up as the one that was just operated on. Very gently you caress the top of your chest, where the scar must be, but what you feel like doesn't feel like a chest. It feels like . . . well, that must be the effects of the operation. He said it would take a while before you felt like your old self. It would help if you could feel more sensation in your legs and feet, you know you can't walk, but if you could just move your legs a little bit.

When you just rubbed your hands together, did you feel anything? Did you feel hands? Why are you so afraid to call out, to find out where you are? You are not in the recovery room. You are not even in the hospital. You are not home. Are you above ground, above the earth, floating in space? There was no white light, no crossing over to the other side, so you are not having an out of body experience. You are not weightless, but you cannot feel a single object. Quietly, gradually, somewhat weirdly, it begins to sink in. You realize you have just died. And on cue, you can now sense that someone or something is coming towards you. Instantly, it pops into your mind—is it a spirit guide? You are not ready for that. You hope it is an old friend or favorite relative. You are aware your heart is beating rapidly. Whatever it is, is almost upon you. Aren't you supposed to be reunited with lost loved ones? But is it true? What in God's name is coming to get you? You are beginning to panic . . .

I'll stop here, the point of no return. Beyond lies the realm of unimaginable supernatural transcendence. It is enough that it is at least conceivable that our consciousness, in some recognizably human, intact form might survive our physical death. For how long—no one can say. It is worth noting that while theologians are almost exclusively preoccupied with the fate of the soul in either heaven or hell, popular accounts of the afterlife are concerned with the far more practical issue of *transition*. It sounds wonderful, if it is true, that a spotlessly clean, idyllic place called heaven, where we are forever comforted, enlightened, transported, at one with infinite cosmic goodness, awaits us. But just how do we get there? Is it painful to physically die? Is the sensation of having our earthly consciousness suddenly snuffed out as horrible as it seems?

Exactly what is that first moment like, for there must be a first moment, when we realize we have died?

My thought experiment is meant to dramatize all those psychological issues that are carefully bypassed in both the theological and popular depictions of the afterlife. If consciousness is to be our starting point, we cannot forget that our initial awareness of death begins with the sick and dying person, the corpse he or she becomes, and the funeral service that follows. No one who has seen a coffin lowered into the ground—of someone with whom they have had any meaningful contact—will easily forget it. We see why fantasies of the afterlife tend to begin well above the corpse in the coffin, above the earth in which it is buried, in the most cloud-filled, spaciously conceivable surroundings. We see why someone, whose consciousness had inexplicably survived their death, would most likely be frightened at their unprecedented transformation. He or she could not help but immediately wonder if they maintained the same physical connection, guaranteed by gravity, to the earth. It is likely they would be desperate for markers of this former existence. Like the infant first exploring how their body interacts with the endlessly novel surrounding world, their new afterlife adult consciousness would want to find out what it means to have died. What kind of a body do they have? Do their five senses still work? Can they feel pain? Speak? Walk? Are there objects with which to interact? Other people? Are they instead, like ghosts, immaterial presences that cannot effect anything material, as often depicted?

It is therefore hard to imagine if their afterlife consciousness is anything like their human predecessor, that within minutes they would not become increasingly anxious and panicky. The novelty of their radical metamorphosis would soon overwhelm them. The realization that they have just lost, by dying, everything they ever loved or valued or been comforted by would be gut-wrenching. The recognition that their only hope would be that somehow, miraculously, they are perhaps going to be inducted into an unimaginably different world, would be terrifyingly daunting to accept.

Such, I believe, is the only logical, psychologically plausible starting place from which the human imagination can realistically begin to contemplate their possible feelings about the afterlife. Not surprisingly, what I have suggested has been thoroughly—except in horror stories—denied and repressed. In its stead, we have the familiar anthropomorphizing of the afterlife. Although we may readily embrace Steven Spielberg's ET as an extraterrestrial playmate, no one, I think, would want to discover that the one and only God bore the appearance and shape of an alien, howsoever adorable.

All of which makes it difficult if not impossible for the ordinary person to determine what they really believe when the question concerns the metaphysical fate of their consciousness or soul. Knowing that science cannot help them here, the temptation will be enormous to be told by some authority what to think and to feel about one of the most perplexing conundrums of their existence. This may be why, in over thirty years of dealing with thousands of patients, I have been repeatedly struck at the poverty of genuine creative thought when it comes to fundamental religious beliefs. Otherwise resourceful, smart, wise, thoughtful, even truly brilliant people can turn mute when the question of the afterlife is raised. This can only be because few of us, unless indoctrinated as children or cornered with life-threatening existential crises, are willing to think about such things. Is this because they lack courage? No, I think, they lack hope. They lack hope because they lack belief, belief that they could survive what they fear will be an unbearable existential exploration. And they lack belief because, crucially, they lack anything that might count as plausible evidence.

Back in the nineteenth century, Nietzsche famously (and it is now apparent very mistakenly) said that God is dead. But he also said very prophetically that people—in a time far more pious than our own—simply do not live as if they really believed in heaven and hell. If they did, they would spend by far the greater part of their waking hours straining heroically to get into heaven. An overriding, religious purpose would dominate their lives. No longer would they be overwhelmed by the world in which they live. What used to be mere flickering transcendental yearnings would slowly coalesce and begin to cast an unbreakable spell.

With the help of another thought experiment, we can imagine such a world in which belief would be supreme. If we can imagine that a God could come down to the earth in the form of a man—a belief that had many predecessors prior to the life of Christ—we can imagine a God desiring to give a wake-up call to a woefully skeptical, secular and sinning world, a last chance, say, before raining down the apocalypse. We might then have . . .

Afterlife Anonymous

You are in a room, a place where those who suffer from incurable skepticism can gather if they choose for healing for one day a year. Whoever comes is guaranteed the same confidentiality that he or she would receive if they attended a meeting of Alcoholics Anonymous. Although it looks ordinary, the room is not. What at first is a dais in front with a long grey table and a curiously empty row of wooden chairs begins to change as soon as the meeting begins. No one can explain how, but all agree that gradually faces, hands, bodies materialize into distinct human beings who once had lived but now are dead. None of them are reappearances of departed loved ones. None of them can be recognized from the recorded pages of history. But all have lived lives, all at one time or another had been skeptics. All have returned from the afterlife to give testimony to their wayward, earthly brothers and sisters. Only two such meeting places of Afterlife Anonymous exist on earth. According to your choice, you can hear testimony from those who presently live in heaven, or those who are in hell. There to inspire and not terrorize their guests, they all speak plainly, all do their best to be reassuring. Each tells an individual tale of cynicism, despair and bottoming out. Those who were lucky enough to redeem themselves, tell how they managed to find the light. Their portrayal of heaven is described over and over again as indescribably joyful. Rather than details, they strive to relay the most common, fundamentally human feelings. They do not deny the divine but they are careful to exclude mention of God the Father, which must be experienced to be believed. Although they do not sound so different than ordinary people who claim to be in daily communion with their God, their testimony, which is seen and heard first hand, carries incomparably more weight. As does their less fortunate brethren who did not make it to heaven, but who, in their own grim way, are as eager to tell their stories of loss. The loss is not of missed opportunities on earth, but of what might have happened in the afterlife. It is not a horror story of burning oil, taunting devils, and medieval torturing. It is the psychic anguish of recognizing once and for all the price that is to be paid for willfully destroying everything that had been precious about their soul . . .

Anyone who can picture the above will see the difference between someone who says he or she really believes in another world—but hardly acts that way—and someone who unquestionably does. If a place such as Afterlife Anonymous really was available, we can imagine the impact. At the very least, there would be an unprecedented explosion of spiritual rebirth. Pursuit of the transcendental world to come would far outstrip pursuit of the materialistic. Science would proceed apace, but the new physics would be more about the paranormal than the number of extra dimensions, the mathematical harmonies of string theory and the mystery of the multiverse. Endless experimentation would ensue to determine the exact nature of the hidden laws of Afterlife Anonymous. Furious scientific and philosophical debates would erupt as to what exactly does the experience prove. That we have definitive proof at last that there is a supreme being who designed the universe? That we are being toyed with, perhaps, by a malicious extraterrestrial who comes from a planet thousands or millions of years more advanced than ours? All would agree, however, that an authentic, supernatural event had occurred. In spite of which, assuming that we had not genetically changed, much of the world would go on as before. Although there would be wannabe saints galore, there would be plenty of sinners. Those who rebelled for the sake of rebelling. Those who cracked under the tension of waiting to learn the eventual fate of their soul. Those who were willing to pay whatever price in order to gratify their darkest impulses.

If these two thought experiments sound oddly fanciful, it is because they deliberately clash with contemporary fantasies of the afterlife. In order to see clearly what people believe, or want to believe about what happens when they die, we do not have to go further than the classic cinematic portrayals of close encounters of the third kind.

Hollywood Heaven

Frank Capra's much beloved 1946 film, *It's a Wonderful Life*, is an unforgettable story of despair and salvation. We see George Bailey (immortally played by Jimmy Stewart) as a young man full of hope, who dreams of traveling the world and doing great things. Just as he is about to leave his hometown of Bedford Falls, fate intervenes. His father unexpectedly dies and his uncle (played by Thomas Mitchell) pleadingly tells him that the only person who can possibly save his father's building and loan association from financial ruin is himself. It is the last thing he had ever wanted to do, but George Bailey cannot abandon his father's legacy. Abandoning his own dreams instead, he steps in and rescues the company. Reluctantly, he decides to marry the hometown girl (impeccably played by Donna Reed), with whom he has fallen in love. He has children. And slowly, insidiously, he becomes increasingly bitter as he is forced to make sacrifice after sacrifice. It is the last straw when Mr. Potter (chillingly played by Lionel Barrymore), the town's robber baron, arranges to have him driven to bankruptcy and falsely accused of fraud. Faced with eight years of jail time, on a snowy Christmas night George Bailey decides to commit suicide by jumping from the Bedford Falls bridge to the icy, swirling waters below.

It is here that one Clarence Oddbody, George Bailey's guardian angel who so far has been a background presence, surveying the arc of his new charge's life, is forced to intervene. Knowing that he would feel compelled to rescue him, assuming human form, he jumps in himself. And is promptly saved by a predictably self-sacrificing George Bailey. Properly introduced at last, Clarence does his best, without much success, to talk him out of his plan to commit suicide. Finally, summing up his profound sense of disappointment in a useless life, he mutters that it would have been better to have "never been born." Suddenly, Clarence gets an angelic inspiration. Why not grant George Bailey his wish, and show him exactly what would have transpired if he really had never been born?

What follows is a ten minute scene that is one of the most famous in cinematic history. A dumbfounded George Bailey is treated to a horrifying alternative version of what life in Bedford Falls would have been like without his presence. He sees how small, seemingly trivial changes, each of which makes perfect sense in itself, leads to a staggering difference. Without George to save it, Bedford Falls has been swallowed up by Mr. Potter's bank and renamed Pottersville. What once was a Normal Rockwell version of small town bliss, now reeks of urban decadence. Bars and pool halls are everywhere. The community of small homes single-handedly financed and kept afloat by George Bailey's building and loan association has literally been replaced by a cemetery.

Far worse, he learns that his uncle, unable to bear the disgrace of bankruptcy, is in an insane asylum. His mother, wizened and cynical, runs a dilapidated boarding house. She does not recognize her own son. His wife has turned into a shriveled, unmarried librarian who screams in terror as George desperately tries to embrace her. He discovers that the two hundred men on the World War II transport ship—who had been rescued from enemy fire by his Medal of Honor winner younger brother—had instead all died. Incredulous, he is reminded by Clarence that his brother, whom George had once rescued from drowning as a child, had of course died in his absence; and so, of course, had the two hundred men he had been destined to save.

It is at this moment that Clarence utters the climactic moving lines in the movie: "Strange, isn't it? Each man's life touches so many other lives, and when he isn't around he leaves an awful hole, doesn't he? . . . You see, George, you really had a wonderful life."

To Stephen Jay Gould in his book, *A Wonderful Life*, these final scenes offer a stunning illustration of his own cherished theory of contingency: that much of what happens in evolution could easily have been otherwise because "small and apparently insignificant changes . . . (can) lead to causes of accumulating differences."

From the standpoint of our theme, however, the movie is a memorable example of the seductive power of wishful thinking. For who wouldn't, when we had reached the end of our rope, want to be rescued by a Clarence Oddbody? Who wouldn't— when we felt most invisible in the eyes of the world—savor seeing a tape of the lives he or she had really touched and of "the awful hole" their absence had left behind?

In Warren Beatty's 1978 remake, *Heaven Can Wait*, the guardian angel has been replaced by a New Age spirit guide, the incredibly patient, hypnotically tranquil, mellifluous-voiced James Mason as Mr. Jordan. Although it is impossible to imagine a less threatening convoy to another world, we see Warren Beatty, the young quarterback who has just died, stubbornly refusing to go. His time just cannot be up, he insists, and somehow he does seem to know that a mistake really has been made. The one (Buck Henry) whose job was to immediately collect the soul of the freshly dead body— underestimating the ability of the super athletic quarterback to swerve his bicycle out of the path of the oncoming vehicle—

had indeed acted prematurely. The quintessence of fairness, Mr. Jordan squarely acknowledges his dilemma. He cannot undo the mistake that has been done on earth, but neither can he bring him to heaven before his appointed time is really up. The compromise solution is to find a different body, a body that has just died, and put Warren Beatty's soul in it. Although his spirit will be his own, his new body will be that of its former owner. In the course of working out the innumerable existential conflicts that crop up between old body and new soul, we are treated to sweet comic turns by Warren Beatty, Charles Grodin and Dyan Cannon. The corniest of feel-good movies, it is irresistibly enjoyable. No one who sees this film, no matter how fervently pious, can possibly take seriously the angel-tempered Mr. Jordan, the lamb-white, heavenly clouds, the ridiculous school yard argument between Warren Beatty and the divine messenger. Knowing it cannot be true and there is nothing to fear, we are free to suspend our disbelief and for a few magic hours indulge our favorite fantasies for cosmic rescue.

On another level, the movie can be viewed as lightheartedly presenting some very disturbing and very real issues. Warren Beatty's refusal to accept he has died, resonates with a universal denial of our death. His incessant bickering with Mr. Jordan symbolizes our sense that, at bottom, life is not fair. His insistence that Mr. Jordan has made an inexcusable mistake reflects our Job-like perception that the suffering we are asked to endure can never be justified. Mr. Jordan's admission of error can be seen as a kind of long overdue apology from the cosmos for the ill treatment we have received. Warren Beatty's restless desire to find the right body for his soul mirrors a universal wish to peek into other people's minds, to secretly observe their lives, to magically break out from the prison of their own identities. (To this degree, *Heaven Can Wait* is a warm and fuzzy predecessor of the much more existentially self-conscious *Being John Malkovich*.)

The reluctance to accept our possible fate as a bodiless soul is depicted in far more penetrating depth in the 1990 mega hit, *Ghost*. Soon after the movie begins, we are witness to the savage murder of Patrick Swayze, a likable yuppie who dies in the arms of his beautiful girlfriend, Demi Moore. We see what looks like a clone of Patrick Swayze rise up from his prostrate, lifeless body. Although it is his ghost, it does not seem to know it. Gradually, as Patrick Swayze sadly stares at the bleeding corpse of his former self, it sinks in that whatever he has just become, it is not something that in any recognizable way is physical. He cannot make contact with the real world. He can see his hysterical girlfriend cradling his head in the deserted alleyway. He can hear her screaming for help. But he cannot touch her. He cannot speak to her. He cannot communicate to her. What he is able to do is to feel the exquisite abandonment of having just lost everything he ever prized about being alive. He can mourn the almost infinite chasm separating the living from the undead. He can know the terror of wondering if perhaps he is the only being residing in this inexplicably altered world.

On the most simple of plot levels, *Ghost* is a New Age spiritual love story: grieving girlfriend is reunited with the loving ghost of her murdered boyfriend. On another level, however, this is a poetically interesting, existential exploration of what it might actually be like to be a legitimate ghost. Much of the appeal of the movie is the way it manages to lure us into an empathic identification with other-worldly challenges now faced by its protagonist. We root for Patrick Swayze as he learns how to walk through walls. We experience his relief when, after numerous trials and errors, he masters the necessary art of telekinesis: by fully accepting his complete absence of corporeality, by focusing only his mind, he can actually move physical objects. We share in his joy when, in a climactic scene—by sending a penny slowly, beautifully floating through air—he manages to convince his skeptical girlfriend that, although she cannot see or hear him, he really does exist.

By the movie's end, he is able to break through and at last communicate with Demi Moore. His parting words, as he ascends to the heavenly white light which seems to beckon him, are: "You know what the most amazing thing is? The love never leaves you. You take it all with you!"

It is what we want to hear. Patrick Swayze, at the height of his *Dirty Dancing* fame when the movie was made, is the ghost many of us would like to become. The anguish at having to die is redirected towards a desperate attempt to save his girlfriend from being murdered by the same man who murdered him. The dread of what might await us in the afterlife, is projected into a paranoid, haunted-looking creature—the first and only fellow ghost he really gets to interact with—who endlessly rides the underground subways (in a vain attempt to prove he did not take his own life by jumping onto the subway tracks, but was pushed instead).

In stark contrast, the small 1997 film, *The Apostle*, is a brutally unsentimental portrayal of a tortured Pentecostal preacher, who is feverishly seeking redemption. Sonny Dewey (brilliantly played by Robert Duvall), enraged by his wife, Jesse's (Farah Fawcett) infidelity, has attacked her lover with a baseball bat. Fearing he has perhaps murdered the now unconscious man, he leaves Texas, ditches his car, and all proofs of his previous identity. Winding up in a small, largely black, Louisiana town, he names himself "The Apostle EF" and dedicates himself to building a new church and a new life. The film seems to go out of its way to show how deeply flawed Sonny Dewey is. Over and over the movie makes the point that he is a womanizer, a drinker and a brawler, a passionately direct but impulse-ridden man who cannot take no for an answer and is clearly, even joyfully prone to violence.

Most mesmerizing of all is the relationship he maintains towards his personal God. When he can no longer tolerate his frustration, he is not above yelling and remonstrating with his Maker, as though he were literally in the same room with him and fully to blame. Watching Robert Duvall we can see (in the words of Edward O. Wilson, describing his own turn as an evangelical teenager), that he had the *power*. Whatever it is he believes or thinks he believes in, there is no doubt he experiences it, feels it in his guts. It pours out of him like a catharsis. It is impossible not to be electrified by the sheer force of his manic belief. It hardly matters what he believes in. It is more than enough to see him singing, chanting, sermonizing, rhythmically clapping his hands. Such faith, he seems to be saying with every fiber of his body, can move mountains.

What his faith cannot do, however, is get him to take a hard, honest look at himself and what he has just done. That in a fit of jealous, drunken rage he (as it turns out) has taken the life of another human being, no more flawed than he is. That he not only shows no remorse for the murder he has committed, but will gloat about it to his friend, "I think I sent him on the way to the glory road."

Sonny Dewey, on fire with the agony and the ecstasy of his love affair with his Savior, does not seem to know there is more to the human heart than just sin and redemption, more than confession and repentance. There is reparation, guilt which arises from empathy for the pain one has caused, there is authentic hard-won change which does not require a payoff in the afterlife.

If *It's a Wonderful Life* and *Ghost* show what it is we wish for when we wish for the afterlife, *The Apostle* shows the kind of wild euphoria that can be attained—if we are willing to suspend all disbelief and surrender all sense of individual accountability.

The Patient's Prayer
or
I Hope Somebody Up There Likes Me

What had begun as a classroom prank had quickly become something else. For some reason Vincent, sitting to my right, had taken offense to the pellets of water randomly flying his way. Although others had laughed, or pretended to, knowing that Lenny, a bit of a bully, was not someone to be confronted, Vincent was having none of it. "What are you doing?" By way of answer Lenny brought his squirtgun a few sadistic inches from his victim's nose and emptied the barrel. "I'm shooting you in the face." I still remember that dumbfounded, panic-stricken look of bottled up rage, shame and helpless, abject fear as though he knew—no matter what he did—he would never live the incident down.

It was the last image I would have of Vincent. I do not remember ever seeing him again. A few months later, after ten dreary years in Bridgeport, Connecticut, my parents moved to the Bronx. Two years later, upon graduating high school, I decided to revisit some friends from my old neighborhood. By chance, one of them had on display the freshly bound graduation album of my former high school. Curious if I could still recognize my classmates, I began leafing through the book. I don't know what I was really looking for, but I could not have imagined encountering Vincent's memorial: the startling black ribbon bordering his young, earnest face; the brief inscription telling the world that Vincent _____ had been killed in a mountain climbing accident.

Instantly, a narrative arc flashed in my mind. To eradicate his shame, to prove his courage, he had recklessly signed on for a mountain climbing expedition for which he was hardly prepared. He had pushed himself to take chances he should never have taken. His act of daring was his final answer to those who had doubted he had the resolve to put himself on the line. Looking at his face one last time, I wondered perhaps if Lenny and his squirtgun, not the treacherous mountain, had been the true culprit in Vincent's demise.

Thirty years later, a patient would tell me about another gruesome mountain climbing accident. His sister's boyfriend, a young English physics student, while climbing a mountain without a companion, had fallen into a crevice from which he could not extricate himself. By the time he was rescued three days later, he had frozen to death. Plainly shaken, my patient could only wonder, "Can you imagine what that must have been like?"

Of all the existential turning points that comprise an individual life, few are greater than the prospect of one's own extinction. And none can match the uncanny sensation of witnessing the actual arrival of one's death. What is it like to know that you are about to fall, that you are falling from a mountain to your certain death? That, stuck in a crack in a mountain, you are slowly and surely freezing to death?

Nothing is more understandable than that people desperately do not want to experience such existential crises alone. It does not matter that such an encounter is something that can only be experienced alone. At such dire times, the prospect of facing our extinction like a brave existentialist offers scant little comfort. Much better is it to try to fan the dying embers of whatever hope seems left, to beg from the universe for one more chance to pray for an eleventh hour intervention of any kind. It could be a ladder from a helicopter, the voice of a rescue team, the handiwork of a guardian angel. At such times no one, not even the most diehard atheist, would turn down the help of a Clarence Oddbody. At such times, when we are overwhelmed with the crushing helplessness of our situation, we want someone, anyone in the world to take note and feel sorry for us. Most often, that kind of empathy implies a feminine spirit. Not surprisingly it was said, after the second World War, that the person most mentioned in the final breaths of the dying soldier was their mother.

A core of religious belief can therefore be understood as the SOS of a very frightened human being to whoever, or whatever in the cosmos may be listening. Although patients do not articulate such feelings in therapy, if I could put their prayers at such times into words, it might be:

> "Someone, something help me.
> My life may not count for much, but it's
> all I've got. Please don't take it away from
> me. I'm not ready. Give me one more
> chance. Do you hear me? Then, help!"

Much of the history of organized religion can be viewed as the various responses that have been offered. All of them, to a greater or lesser degree, come down to this:

> "You are not alone. Help is on the way.
> This is what you have to do, this is where
> you have to go to get it."

The question and answer, it is obvious, speak to a primal need. A related, but far different question, one that can only be ignored at our peril, is:

"Is it true?"

CHAPTER TWO

WHEN BAD THINGS HAPPEN TO GOOD PEOPLE

When Aaron Kushner stopped gaining weight at the age of eight months, his parents became concerned. When his hair started falling out after he turned one year old, they began taking him to specialists. Their son's condition, they would eventually be told, was called progeria, "rapidly aging." Aaron, it seemed, would grow to about three feet in height. He would have no hair on his head or body. While still a child, he would begin to look like a little old man. He would die in his early teens.

It was the kind of tragedy for which Harold Kushner, a young rabbi who was already the head of a local congregation in a suburb of Boston, had been trained to handle. A religious man all his life who had never doubted the existence of God, the goodness of God, the wisdom of God, it was his job to explain the inexplicable. To the families of dying children whose lives had been cut short before they had really begun. To the mother of the little girl who had been run over by a bus on the way home from school. To the woman whose body slowly but surely, one function after another, was being crippled by multiple sclerosis. The answers he offered were the answers he had always believed. Whatever happens, happens for a purpose. Although it may look otherwise now, virtue will be rewarded and wickedness will be punished. The righteous will be protected.

For those who hold their faith, the goodness of the world will surely one day be revealed.

So it would be for Harold Kushner in his darkest hour. He had been nothing if not a good man. His life was one of service. His faith in God was the center of his being. It was not possible that his God would abandon him. But as the months and years wore on, as the progeria more and more took hold of the son whom he adored, something began to change. The consolations that were his stock and trade, that he had always relied upon, he now began to question. For the first time he found himself seriously rethinking his core beliefs. When his friends and colleagues would offer traditional words of comfort, the grief counseling at which he was so adept, he became increasingly skeptical. How could it be that he could have possibly "deserved" what had happened to his son? That it had somehow been "for his own good"? That he must remember "the redemptive value of suffering." That human beings, no matter how religious, are simply "not capable of understanding God's ways." That "no one has the right to question God's will" and his own favorite chestnut, that "everything has a purpose."

When Bad Things Happen To Good People is Harold Kushner's deeply felt, personal answer to what is traditionally called The Problem of Evil: how is it possible for an all-good, all-wise, all-powerful God to tolerate the existence of evil? His book is remarkable for how frankly it acknowledges his anger at his God for punishing him unfairly. He cannot and will not accept the standard consolations his religion offers. There can be no justification, he finally decides, for a God to willingly give cancer to a child, progeria to his son, a brain tumor to an innocent woman. A God who could do that would have to be evil. But God, of course, cannot be evil. There would be no meaning to the world if that were true. If such a God existed, he would not want to believe in Him.

It is at this crossroads in his faith that Harold Kushner makes a daring choice. Deciding that a God who is all good and all powerful could never willfully punish an innocent child, he arrives at the radical conclusion that God is *not omnipotent*. God does not want, never wants bad things to happen to good people. God always wants to help, but he *cannot always control what happens*. God, therefore, Harold Kushner triumphantly asserts, does *not* cause suffering or withhold cures for cancer or any other horrible disease.

What is the basis for the revolutionary claim that God—in opposition to two thousand years of theological doctrine—is not omnipotent? His main reason, as he is honest enough to admit, is simply that "It can't be there is no God . . . (there would then) be no purpose to life." He is fortified in his new belief by a physicist who tells him that at the heart of quantum mechanics is the principle of indeterminacy. To Harold Kushner this means that even God—who undoubtedly created both Heaven and earth, and all that is in it—cannot predict and therefore cannot control certain undesirable events. It follows that God cannot control certain pockets of local events, such as who will contract a particular disease, who will have their life cut short by a tragic accident, who will become the next unlucky victim of a deranged serial killer. God does not want suffering, he does not want disease, but he is unable to control the fate (because of quantum mechanics) of every single atom in the universe which He created. And when bad things happen to good people, God feels as bad about it as we do.

Encouraged and inspired by these ideas, which have taken him years to arrive at, he goes on to construct his own personalized, secular theology. Although he is at pains to acknowledge he is neither philosopher nor theologian, his ideas strike one as being both heartfelt and intriguingly innovative. He believes in prayer, but he does not believe in praying for a divine intervention. God cannot control the details of the future (presumably again because of quantum mechanics). But prayer helps, because it puts us in touch with the presence, the goodness of God. It reminds us that God loves us, thinks constantly about our well-being and is rooting for us. He points out that not all suffering is bad. He asks rhetorically if we would really want to live in a world without pain, without hardship, without struggle? Would it not be boring to live forever? It is wrong to do things—not because we want to—but because we are seeking a reward in the afterlife. Although he personally believes that the soul is eternal, who can really know what lies in store for us after we die? More important is it that we count our blessings on earth and give thanks for the goodness that God has put everywhere around us. Not all parts of the Bible, he warns us, are to be taken literally. When it says in the Book of Genesis that "first there was water, then land, then . . ."— since that has been subsequently confirmed by modern earth science—we are right to take it not only literally but as one more sign of divine wisdom. When it says that the world was created in six days, we are to understand that the statement is merely a metaphor.

No challenge is greater to the believer who wants to defend the goodness of God than the history of the genocides that have been perpetuated. Harold Kushner's explanation for why God allowed Hitler to kill six million Jews rests on the supposed necessity for free will. If there were no free will, it could not be just to punish the wicked and reward the virtuous. If a mother does not allow her child to make a mistake, if the child chooses the right path only because he or she has to, there is no free will. Analogously, if God is to allow all people, even a demented, evil genius like Adolf Hitler to have free will, he cannot intercede.

That, of course, does not mean, as Kushner is quick to emphasize, that God wants Hitler to kill six million Jews for some higher purpose (as a punishment, perhaps, for a heinous lapse into heathen secularism). No, God once again is as grief-stricken as we are, but He has no choice but to wait and see what happens.

I must admit at this point I find it incredible that Rabbi Kushner, an obviously good man, can believe this. How can it be possible that a God, powerful enough to create molecular biology, quantum mechanics and general relativity physics, can think of nothing to even slow down a process of genocide? Why is it necessary for God to wait patiently as Hitler systematically kills each and every Jew before he can begin to punish him? Once Hitler has made the decision to exterminate the Jews—penned the order, say, to carry out the infamous "final solution"—isn't that freedom enough to choose evil? Why can't God stop him at that point? A moment's thought shows it is not true that a person needs to complete an act before he or she can be said to choose. Suppose someone in cold blood, deciding to murder an innocent person, has taken a gun and just squeezed the trigger? Hasn't he chosen? Why can't God at that moment, or at any of an infinite number of possible intermediate points between the inauguration of the evil act and its completion, intervene—when intervention is what is desperately needed? When people are about to become victims of unconscionably brutal crimes, they do not pray to their God to respect the free will of their would-be predator. They pray for exactly the same thing that a hurt or frightened child wants when they run to their parents—for immediate hands-on help. And if Kushner is right, if it is existentially imperative that we respect the right—of good people and evil people alike—to exercise their free will, shouldn't truly religious people not only be pacifists, but refuse to intercede in someone's commission of even the most monstrous act? To stand by and not even dial 911 because that might interfere with the God-given right to choose evil? (Imagine someone who actually lived by such a code. Would there be anyone who did not consider them a monster?)

I do not doubt that Harold Kushner would be the first to abjure such absurd conclusions to be drawn from his ideas. Yet, I believe, they follow quite logically for anyone who takes him at his word, carefully thinks through the consequences and then looks at the outcome. He says that free will is necessary in the world. If he really believed that, he would not be so concerned about the adverse effects of early education. He would recognize that although Western jurisprudence is certainly based on coercive ideas of punishment and reward, of deterrence and containment, when free will is at the stake—as Dostoevsky so famously pointed out in *Notes From the Underground*—the evil, perverse man will do exactly as he wants, in spite of (or because of, in defiance of) the consequences. He would realize that to allow free will to exist is not the same thing as allowing crimes to be committed; that free will means freedom to *choose*, not freedom to recklessly carry out shameless acts. Harold Kushner says that sometimes things (meaning inexplicably bad things) happen for no reason at all. They happen randomly. He does not seem to grasp that physicists who talk about the quantum mechanical principle of indeterminacy are not talking about the macroscopic world of people and three-dimensional objects (the only world we care about). They are talking about the sub-atomic world of electrons and quarks, invisible, curled up, extra dimensions, matter and anti-matter, energy and dark energy, the four fundamental forces of the universe and so on. And that in the people-scaled, three-dimensional world we have always lived in, determinism and predictability hold sway to a breathtaking degree of accuracy (if it were otherwise, there could not be such a thing as, for example, rocket science, and the quest to land a man on the moon would not have been accomplished in a million years).

It therefore hardly makes sense that a God who could create the laws of quantum mechanics and general relativity theory, which in turn created the cosmos, who could single-handedly mastermind the Big Bang, could be as powerless to deter the ravages of disease as Harold Kushner is forced to claim. Even if God can't predict every single random act of bad luck, how could He not be responsible for creating plagues such as cancer and AIDS? And if He can't exactly control and predict, why can't He at least make some kind of contribution to the cure for major illnesses? Harold Kushner says God feels as bad as he does, and is as blameless as he is, that his son was afflicted with progeria. Yet, one wonders, if so, just what did He do to help? Did He somehow communicate to Harold Kushner, deliver a message of some kind, containing invaluable advice? Did He hint at a cure for progeria that was at least somewhat ahead of its time?

So my dilemma is that on the one hand, I cannot quite accept that Harold Kushner, a thoughtful, philosophically minded, sincere man, can believe what he says; while on the other hand I am well aware that he does believe it. Why? Because he wants to believe. Because he believes in belief. Because he cannot accept the alternative, as he freely admits—that a God who had the power to prevent bad things happening to good people, and did not, could not be all good. Rather than accept that, he would cling to the seemingly absurd position that an almost (except for quantum mechanics) omnipotent, all-good God has no more ability to contain or eliminate evil than human beings do.

Harold Kushner, it appears, cannot take the next logical step. Maybe God not only cannot cure cancer and cannot prevent evil, but He can't create heaven and earth either. Maybe, if He does exist, it is more like a symbol in the collective unconscious and does not really resemble the concrete picture presented in the Bible. But life would not be meaningful for Harold Kushner were he to believe that, as he often says. Fortunately, he is free to conduct his life on earth as he sees fit. If he is mistaken and will one day be held accountable, according to his beliefs, it will not be until the afterlife. Yet, as he has remarked, he is not really sure what the afterlife is anyway. Because he can think of no way to test his assumption, he is free to believe in whatever he feels he has to believe in. There are no real consequences. Tellingly, he has arrived at a philosophical position in which *the God that he believes in is indistinguishable (by his own criteria) from a God who does not exist.*

The impression remains that nothing could really shake Harold Kushner's faith. If the Holocaust didn't, if September 11 didn't, if all the pogroms carried out against the Jews in the past two thousand years didn't, what would? A War of the Worlds? The faith, it seems, of Harold Kushner is indispensable—as is true of just about all deeply religious people. They would no more change their religion than they would change their sexual orientation. When Harold Kushner says "It can't be there is no God . . . (there would then be) no purpose to life," he seems to be saying "I won't accept that." If you take that refusal, add an abstract space where anything is allowed, that can neither be proved nor disproved, where the deepest, most wishful fantasies can quietly collect unmolested by the constraints of mundane reality, you are likely to arrive at some kind of concept of a personal God.

In short, Harold Kushner believes that everything good in life comes from God. Everything beneficial and healing in culture, education, and parental support, everything motivational and inspirational comes from God. God is pure love. God is not cruel, is not judgmental, is not frustratingly difficult to comprehend. Because He is unable despite his majestic powers to prevent bad things from happening to good people, He is to be held totally blameless and innocent. But we are to remember He is always there, always present as a kind of a cosmic, spiritual, super-parental force wanting nothing but the best for us.

Harold Kushner does not seem to care that he is preaching to the converted. The only proof that he offers in support of his remarkable, revisionist, personal theology is his lifelong feeling of contact with God's love and His presence. He does not seem to consider that few people—who do not already believe in most of what he says—could ever find it convincing.

Perhaps the most disturbing aspect, for me, of *When Bad Things Happen To Good People*, is the implicit conception it conveys of Jehovah as a clearly tribal God (an us-against-them God). Over and over again injustice and unfairness are portrayed as bad things happening to good people. The implication is that it is *not unjust* for bad things to happen to bad people. But why is it okay for anyone to get progeria, for an infant to get Down syndrome, or AIDS, or cancer? How does that fit with a supposedly infinitely good and merciful God? What is the necessity for there being punishment for bad people? Why not loving, nurturing discipline instead? How could an eternity in hell, if hell exists, ever be rationalized (as it was for nearly two thousand years) as the merciful act of a just God? Why wouldn't justice be, say, a day in hell? Or at least no more than the equivalent number of evil hours spent during a lifetime? All of which points to the existence of the Talion law—and eye for an eye and a tooth for a tooth—characteristic of a vengeful, tribal God. As has been often pointed out, the Bible makes it clear that there is a double standard of morality that applies in the first case to the Chosen People and in the second to the converts of the new religion of Christianity. Everyone else, which is most of the rest of the world, are more or less consigned to either eternal damnation or the most savage, earthly retaliation.

What is most valuable about Harold Kushner's book is that it helps people to release and to find a place for their anger. It is for those who already believe but who have been disappointed and hurt by life, who hate what they consider God's unfairness, but who are not ready to give up their religion and don't know what to do with their resentment.

The bitterness that Rabbi Kushner felt and overcame resonates in a strange way with my patients. Although few of them would ever dedicate themselves to religious service, all of them, to a greater or lesser degree, would feel cheated by life. All of them, whatever their religious beliefs, would feel that bad things happen constantly to good people, that life is unfair, that life is hard, that life is unforgiving and that justice, whatever that is, is almost never evenly distributed. If I had only one book in the Bible to represent their unconscious philosophy of life, it would be the Book of Job.

The Skeptical Child

When I was five and just days after my family had moved to Bridgeport, Connecticut, I was introduced to anti-Semitism. Just in case I thought I was fooling anybody, I was reminded that it was known that they all knew "I was a Jew." No other explanation was needed and I understood that was because being Jewish was the same thing as being bad. But why? My father's answer to that, and all such racial taunts, was a defiant and not-too-convincing, "I'm a Jew and proud of it." My mother's was a kind of muttering, angry despair.

But Bobby had been different. Right from the start he and his parents had seemed comfortable with the new family that had moved in a few houses away. It didn't hurt that he was Italian, the ethnic affiliation, according to my mother, that most resembled the Jews, and that for some reason he instinctively looked up to me. We became immediate friends. So on a snowy Christmas Eve about a year later, when I was almost seven and he was about to become six—and I had just been shocked to hear that Bobby still believed that Santa Claus, while he was asleep, would deliver the toys he knew he would find under the family tree in the morning—I had to set him straight.

"Your parents put your toys under the Christmas tree, Bobby."

"No they don't. Santa Claus does."

"There's no such thing as Santa Claus."

"Yes there is. My parents told me."

"They tell that to little kids before they grow up."

Six was too old to believe in fairy tales, and I wanted to believe that I was doing Bobby a favor. It did not occur to me that I felt rejected by Christmas, by the presents I would never receive, by the festive celebrations that did not include me and that far from puncturing a foolish myth, I had set in motion a complicated and ugly chain of events. A few days later my mother would tell me that Bobby's mother, who was very upset, had wanted to know why I had done what I had done. I don't know what answer my mother gave. I don't know what answer I would have given, if they had asked me. All I cared about was that a tension had sprung up between Bobby and myself, a tension that seemed to escalate and would culminate one afternoon in a horrible accusation:

"The Jews killed Christ."

My father's defense—when I reported the crime for which I had just been charged—was instantaneous and bristling: "Tell him, Christ was a Jew."

The new revelation would dismay Bobby even more than my debunking of Santa Claus. At almost seven, I had learned a precious but invaluable lesson. There is little joy in being the bearer of skeptical tidings, especially when the subject is religion. Although we would continue to be friends for the next ten years, it would be the last conversation we would ever have on the rituals of Christmas, the historical role of the Jews in the crucifixion of Christ, the rites and ceremonies that went into living the life of a Catholic or Jew. When his sister received her first communion, I would be the last to know. No matter how many times I saw him get into the family car and leave for Sunday church, he would never mention it. Nor would I talk about what it was like to fast for a whole day on Yom Kippur, to go to a synagogue on the high holy days, to live in a strict Kosher home, to be mandated to attend Hebrew school for two years in order to prepare to be properly Bar Mitzvahed.

To say, as my father would, "I'm a Jew and proud of it," hardly seemed to sum up the experience of growing up Jewish in Bridgeport, Connecticut. I had been forced at a young age to realize there were serious consequences for anyone who was outside the pale of the dominant religious group and I had learned the hard way that what was never spoken about was often what was most important.

That would change, of course, when I was sixteen and I moved with my family to the Bronx, New York. Gone was the need to say one was proud to be Jewish, because it was all too obvious that it was in to be Jewish, that being Jewish automatically meant you were smart and not dumb, that you were different in a quirky and interesting way, funny and warm-hearted, someone who would root for the underdog but would have opportunities galore to be one of life's winners. The only glitch was that none of it seemed particularly real to me. I was no less an outsider now that I was at least nominally and ethnically an insider than when I had lived in Bridgeport, Connecticut. Perhaps I had grown too accustomed to being an introspective loner and a fascinated observer. I loved puzzles of thought, existential quandaries, imagination-driven reveries and, above all, questions about the meaning of life. Nor was it difficult to meet like-minded, wannabe existentialists, who were willing to exuberantly examine philosophical conundrums for which there could be no possible answers. In NYU as an undergraduate, I would learn and begin to articulate for the first time the dark side, the slippery slope of skepticism that went from honest doubt, to cynicism, to indecisiveness, to despair. In the person of my freshman philosophy professor, the celebrated iconoclast Paul Edwards, I would encounter my first activist atheist, and in William Barrett, author of the classic *Irrational Man*, I would experience in the flesh a foremost American existentialist. It was a revelation to realize that the explorations of a daring and uncompromising intellect by no means led to happiness, peace of mind or even emotional stability. If it guaranteed anything, it was in the famous phrase of Jean Paul Sartre, a kind of lingering "painful lucidity" of consciousness.

Despite its dark side, my initial encounter with skepticism was nothing if not liberating. Fortified with my new ideas, I was able to ask my mother (very politely, of course) for the very first time why she believed in God. Bemused at my question,

that I had actually found it necessary to raise it, she smiled
indulgently: "Why, Jerry, when you look at the stars, at the sky,
at everything around us, don't you think that only God could
have made this?" It was the same answer that a religious
butcher—knowing that his regular customer, Paul Edwards,
was also a prominent skeptical philosopher—had personally
offered. It was the answer that Paul Edwards, himself, one
afternoon—while reviewing the standard philosophical
rebuttals to the theologian's traditional arguments purporting
to prove the existence of God—had conceded was the most
personally persuasive, from a purely emotional standpoint.

It was the question I would continue to raise, whenever I got
the chance, for the rest of my life. To my father, systematically
being crippled by congestive heart failure and nearing the end
of his life, I gingerly asked (not knowing what he would say)
what he thought about the afterlife. It took only a moment to
reflect and he had the answer: "When they put you in the
ground six feet under, and throw dirt on you, I think that is it."
To my older sister, who had always countered my skepticism
with her own stubbornly unwavering branch of New Age
spiritualism—who, curiously, a year later, just after throwing
real dirt upon my father's grave, had said, "I'll see you"—against
my better judgment, I wanted to know if her words meant what
I thought they meant. She told me they did and her exasperated
look added that the question had not only been annoying but
redundant. To my financial adviser, a jovial, rotund,
conscientious man whom I have never seen without a yarmulke
on his crown, I brought up the unspoken topic of a Jewish
heaven. Did he believe in one? Had he ever heard of one?
Surprisingly, although he had spent his entire life going to
religious schools, he did not seem to have given the matter any
thought. There might be such a thing. It wasn't talked about.

Did he believe in an afterlife then? Well, it was possible. Perhaps . . . There was a soul, he thought, but the thrust of his Jewish upbringing had clearly emphasized one's conduct on earth.

It was a striking contrast to the rock solid belief system of the Jamaican, born-again Christian woman who occasionally cleaned the office in which I worked. There was no religious question for which she did not have the answer. Heaven and hell existed, of course, but you could not get into heaven if you did not accept Christ. Once you did, the spirit of God is forever with you, forever guiding you. God loves us, but He is also angry at us because of our sins, and that is why the world is surely about to end very soon. The signs of an apocalypse were everywhere. She was not afraid. At seventy-five, after losing two husbands and two sons, she was tired of being a cleaning lady and was looking forward to meeting her Maker. Although I could see she took it for granted she had a ticket to heaven, the fate of my own soul was another story. God would be destroying the wicked when He returned to earth, but He would also be taking some "serious Jews" aside—here she looked pointedly at me—and perhaps would be sparing them (in other words, if I converted now, I would be saving myself a lot of grief later on).

The issue of conversion illustrated a cardinal difference between the Christian and the Jewish religious teaching. If there was no person on earth who was not a potential convert to Christ, it seemed only someone born Jewish was to be considered Jewish. While a technical procedure does exist for the conversion of non-Jews, it was a procedure that was, if at all possible, discouraged. (A Jewish patient, who had married an Asian woman, who was quite willing to change her faith, found it necessary to make one appointment after another with a plainly reluctant rabbi who always seemed to be cancelling.)

When I first arrived in New York City, and first rode the underground subway train, I had also been introduced to my first religious zealot. A tall, somber-looking man, who had been peacefully holding the subway pole while staring into space, had out of the blue begun to scream. A deafening tirade against "the black prince," an unspeakably bestial creature who was the personification of everything that was evil, sinful, slimy and depraved in the sinkhole that was New York City. It was the black prince, the black prince in each of us that would draw down on us the wrath of God, that would deliver us to eternal damnation, that would surely make us burn in hell. That was the gist of his sermon, which went on unabated for the duration of my ride. To my utter dismay, no one in the car seemed to take particular notice of him, his noxious unwanted presence as efficiently erased as those famous instances in which crowds of New Yorkers will silently and quickly walk by as though oblivious to the man or woman lying utterly prostrate on the pavement before them.

Green and young as I was, I could not do that. What was it, I wondered, that was torturing him and why was he screaming to a car full of strangers? Was that the only way he thought he could break through the complacent defenses of hardened sinners? Did he really think, by behaving this way, he was somehow doing God's work? It was obvious he was out of his mind, but what was so meaningful about his religious beliefs that he was willing to risk incarceration in a psychiatric ward in order to publicize them?

In the decades that followed, being a daily subway commuter, I would see hundreds and hundreds of itinerant preachers, impromptu evangelists, born-again Christians, would-be apostles, call them what you will. They preached with a Bible in one hand or cited their favorite scripture from memory. They dressed either as ordinary people who occasionally worked at regular jobs, or as disenfranchised, directionless souls who may or may not have been temporarily homeless. They seemed, to a greater or lesser degree, tormented, agitated, and angry. For someone who was banking his or her entire life on the teachings of Christ, they seemed remarkably bereft of empathy, kindness, compassion, mercy or any discernible goodwill towards their fellow man. They showed no interest and did not display the slightest consideration for the captive audience to whom they grandiosely and belligerently preached.

Later in life, I would realize that the conversion experience (which I will explore in detail in a later chapter) of a serious, mature person can be a rather profound, life-changing event. But here I simply want to contrast the earthbound, secular, common sense philosophizing (in spite of his subsequent wishful thinking, revisionist theology) of someone such as Harold Kushner to its mystical antithesis: the fanatically ideological, no-prisoners-taken, transcendentally-enraptured evangelist.

Enter Rick Warren, author of the sensational, 40 million-copy best-selling *The Purpose Driven Life*, and charismatic, founding pastor of the world famous Saddleback Church in Lake Forest, California. Meant to be a blueprint for a New Age type of grassroots fundamentalism, the book offers a radically pared-down, Alcoholics Anonymous style program for achieving a soul-cleansing, life-altering, "forty day spiritual journey." Except here, there are only five steps (or purposes) that are necessary. Purpose #1: "You were planned for God's pleasure." Purpose #2: "You were formed for God's family." Purpose #3: "You were created to become like Christ." Purpose #4: "You were shaped for serving God." Purpose #5: "You were made for a mission."

Although Rick Warren claims that the sole authority for everything he says derives from the thousand-odd scripture quotations that sprinkle his book, he freely admits that he has taken the liberty to paraphrase and reinterpret whenever necessary. Thus we get (p. 23), "You are not an accident," which he backs up with, "You saw me before I was born and scheduled each day of my life before I began to breathe. Everything was recorded in your book (meant to be taken literally as: "God mixed and matched your parents' DNA for the express purpose of producing you"). In stark contrast to Harold Kushner, the thrust of *The Purpose Driven Life* is towards the afterlife. Everything on earth is designed to guide you to Heaven and the everlasting presence of God.

Although not what the author had in mind, this book was a small revelation to me. Granting that Rick Warren means what he says, I found it astounding that anyone else, let alone 40 million people, could take it seriously. There was not even a shadow of an attempt to address possible doubts to his incredibly sweeping pronouncements. Preaching, it seems, comes as naturally to him as breathing. He needs no other authority than that of divine revelation as revealed to the prophets in the Bible. It does not occur to him that such divine revelations throughout recorded history have been subjected to thousands and thousands of diverse interpretations. Nor is it necessary. Rick Warren, with his unique blend of New Age spiritualism and feel-good fundamentalism, is an indisputable world-beating success, a quintessential example of what it means to be preaching to the converted. In his universe, skeptical thinking has been swept away and doubt does not exist. In the beginning of the book, he tells of having written to 250 leading philosophers, scientists and thinkers and asking each of them, "What is the meaning of life?" He reports that, to a man or woman, they were generally stumped, sometimes even admitting that the best they could do would be to "just guess." They were stumped, according to the author, because they did not realize that the source of true knowledge does not derive from disembodied, abstract thought. It comes from belief in God. It comes from being open to the divine revelation imparted by the biblical prophets. The meaning of life, therefore, can only be found in God's special purpose for us and the shortest path to that is evangelical faith.

In *Steps To An Ecology Of Mind*, Gregory Bateson talked about what he called "third level assumptions." There was learning, there was learning about learning (or learning from our mistakes) and then there was unconscious criteria by which we determine what is to count as learning in the first place and what is not to count. That was the third level assumption. It was Gregory Bateson's contention that such an unconscious filtering device is of prime importance, is developed early on and is extremely hard (especially when maladaptive) to uproot or modify.

So, what is the third level assumption of the evangelical flock to whom Rick Warren so ardently and mightily preaches? It is that unquestioning acceptance of Christ as our Lord is the ticket to eternal life. That the Bible contains the word of God. That our destination will be salvation or damnation. It is the faith of Sonny Dewey, "The Apostle EF" in the climactic last scene— indomitably singing the praises of his Savior as he toils on a prison road gang—and it is awesome to see.

But what are the psychological roots of such blind and passionate belief that literally can hijack the mind?

Freud, Jung and Job

Although he would freely confess that he never personally experienced "the oceanic feeling," Freud did not hesitate to tackle the spiritual longings of the human psyche. In *The Future of an Illusion*, Freud points to the helplessness of the infant who literally cannot survive without the protection of the father and likens it to the adult's helplessness against the forces of nature. God is the cosmic father who protects the adult and, seen this way, religion at bottom is a desperately needed defense. To achieve this, there must be a "humanization of nature": the bestial forces of animism must be turned into gods and polytheism must be consolidated into monotheism. Only then could there be reinstated "the intimate needs and relations between the helpless child/infant and the father/God in full detail." Only then could the same childish need for protection against overwhelming threats—which continues to exist in the adult—be similarly satisfied. And because religious ideas are fulfillments of the "oldest, strongest and most urgent wishes of mankind," they are, according to Freud, "illusions." They are teachings about reality which tell one something one has not discovered for oneself and which lay claim to one's belief. They are attempts to personify nature in order to control it: "psychical mastery as a preparation for physical mastering."

Because we both yearn for the Father's protection and fear His punishment, ambivalence is a hallmark of the religious attitude. Freud seems to be basing his ideas on the origin of God—by using the Old Testament Jehovah as an almost exclusive prototype—and for all practical purposes ignoring the New Testament Christ figure. In the final analysis, not surprisingly,

Freud will turn to psychology to understand God. Religious ideas are illusions. Illusions are not errors; they may in fact be true, but they derive from wishes and that is a poor basis to base anything on. Religion, he therefore famously concludes, is the "universal obsessional neurosis" of humanity and, like the obsessional neurosis of children, it arises out of the Oedipal relation to the father. The believer who therefore accepts the universal neurosis (of religion) is spared the task of constructing a personal one. That is the good news. The bad news is that by the time the child has learned to think independently the teachings of religion will have become ineradicable.

It was Freud's hope, however, that, just as children grow out of a similar neurosis, mankind will eventually overcome the (to him) neurotic stage of religion. He concludes with one of his most frequently quoted sayings: "the voice of the intellect is a soft one, but it does not rest till it has gained a hearing."

Freud lived as he preached. He would endure seventeen cancer operations in his palette in the last years of his life, but he would remain until the very end—according to his physician, Max Schur, in his moving book, *Freud, Living and Dying*—an indomitable skeptic. He never asked for a pain killer stronger than aspirin. Although he did not mention Job, he accepted hardship with a stoicism worthy of a Biblical prophet.

Another genius with a very different philosophy of religion was the great disciple and eventual rival of Freud, Carl Jung. *Answer to Job*, according to many, was his masterwork on the subject. Unlike Freud, Jung is both perplexed and fascinated by his subject. He states frankly in the preface that he does not want to bruise sensibilities and he is fearful of the public's reaction. He appears worried that his views—especially on the touchy subject of the problem of evil—may be considered too heretical.

He begins by saying that religious numina are autonomous. They are not created by man. They come whole cloth, revealing themselves in dreams and various conversion experiences. They cannot be reduced to scientific measurement, and are therefore not susceptible to proof. True religion is about meaning—not miracles—although miracles sometimes reveal it. You don't, however, need miracles, and if you do, you don't understand religion.

Throughout the book, Jung struggles to unify the profound inconsistencies and ethical lapses of (what to him is) the savage tribal God of the Old Testament with the world-weary conscience of the modern world (faced, for example, with explaining genocides such as the Holocaust). At times the picture he draws—almost one of a schizoid God striving for unity—seems eerily akin to the impassioned but self-doubting religious meditations of a William James.

Unlike Freud, Jung wants to replace the psychodynamics and cognitive unconscious with his own archetypal vision of a collective unconscious. Because he wrote in a time when it was agreed that certain domains of subjectivity—the descriptive unconscious, spirituality, transcendentalism—were forever beyond the reaches of experimental, physical science, he did not see the need for proof. That imaginary wall, however, thanks to contemporary neuroscience, is rapidly crumbling.

Like Harold Kushner, however, Jung cannot let go of the God archetype. Like Harold Kushner, Jung agonizes over the problem of evil posed by Job. Like Harold Kushner, Jung finds resolution in a flawed God—in his case a God divided, at odds with Himself, who suffers a kind of Biblical version of split personality.

In hindsight we can perhaps see that once we free ourselves from the emotional compulsion that life cannot be meaningful unless the Bible were literally true, we remove a kind of theological straightjacket. It becomes possible to have spirituality and mysticism without the necessity of believing in ancient miracles. It is not true the skeptic needs genuine hope, hope that uplifts, less urgently than the evangelist. It is just that he is more discriminating.

In a sense, the history of religion has been the record of their various answers to the problem of Job, which is the problem of evil. It is the problem no patient of mine—although they almost never use the word evil—has ever been able to resolve.

One other problem no patient has been able to solve is how to deal with the fact of their death.

CHAPTER THREE

DEATH AND DYING

In 1965 four divinity students of the Chicago Theological Seminary approached a young and then unknown psychiatrist with a novel request. Could she help them with a research project they were planning on the processes of dying? Could she perhaps guide them to the relevant data they would need?

The idea, clicking at once with Elizabeth Kübler-Ross, she decided to interview a dying patient the following week, with the students being permitted to silently watch. The plan seemed straightforward and simple enough, but to her great surprise, in spite of her persistent attempts, she would not get a single chance to even get near such a patient. Doctors either changed the subject, avoided her, expressed disbelief she could be so insensitive as to even think of such an idea, or refused to concede they even knew of a patient who was dying. Ironically, Elizabeth Kübler-Ross was left to wonder if it were possible there could actually be no dying patients in a gigantic modern hospital.

Eventually a hospital chaplain would come to her aid, a cooperative, dying patient would be found and an initial interview would be successfully conducted. From such inauspicious beginnings, two and one half years later a modern classic of psychiatry—*On Death and Dying*—would be born and a worldwide movement in thanatology would be launched. Her celebrated five stages of dying—denial and isolation; anger;

bargaining; depression and acceptance—thenceforth to be endlessly quoted by professional and layman alike, would enter the language and seem destined for immortality. And forty years later, reading her today, her fundamental insights, common sense wisdom and above all indomitable spirit, still come across as prescient. Magically, right from the start she exudes the unerring confidence of the true pioneer. She knows somehow she is more aware than anyone else in the world of the importance of confronting one's impending death with dignity. She knows she cannot help her patients reach the final stage of acceptance if she herself is frightened of dying. She knows she cannot display the empathy for the terminally ill person that is so crucial, if she cannot conquer her own fears.

Written with hypnotic, deceptive simplicity, *On Death and Dying* can leave an indelible mark on the receptive reader. Although I thought it was both a masterful and moving book, I have to admit it was the kind of book I literally couldn't wait to finish. The unbroken, unrelieved exposure to the sorrow and suffering of forlorn, terminally ill patients eventually took their toll and became suffocating. Reading the book, I alternately heard two voices in my head: one said, this is wonderful; the other said, how much more of this can I take?

At the heart of Elizabeth Kübler-Ross's book, and from the standpoint of our theme, I felt was a conundrum. On the one hand she had been braver and more eloquent than others in exposing and confronting our deep-seated, human-all-too-human denial of death. She had been an advocate for patients' rights long before it became fashionable. When few would listen, she had sounded the alarm against the growing compartmentalization and dehumanization of the medical establishment. On the other hand, there were at times an ambivalence and an underlying mysticism that could belie her otherwise impeccable scientific rigor. She could frankly say at one point—of a frightened, dying patient's mention of the afterlife—"this is denial." She could dryly comment of another patient, "No one can deny all the time." She could proudly state that all but two of her patients would wind up accepting death. But she could also say at another point—of a lonely, dying patient's glaring lack of a comforting family—that her denial of death in this case was contributed to by the absence of "a sound religious upbringing." According to her, traditional religion could therefore either collude with the denial of death or it could dispel it. I had to wonder why, from the very beginning of her researches, hospital chaplains had been conspicuously present on her team. Was this an administrative necessity, a response to a patient's request or was it the expression of her own personal need?

A decade after I first read her book, and late into her career, I happened to see a television interview with Elizabeth Kübler-Ross. Unhurried in her manner, seemingly deep at peace within herself, she spoke with an almost eerie authority. "Anyone who works with the dying," she said quietly, "quickly comes to lose their fear of death." In subsequent interviews, she would speak about patients who had undergone out-of-body, near-death experiences. She would note that the remarkable similarity of their reports could hardly be explained by coincidence. More and more it seemed she was edging towards an acceptance of the afterlife. Towards the end of her life, it was reported, after delving deeper and deeper into an exploration of the supernatural, she had embraced an outright, mystical view of life. She had gone from being a guide to the dying, to being a guide to the afterlife, someone who would talk boldly of the angel spirits who would come for the souls of the newly dead. Not surprisingly, it was said—at whatever hospital she would visit—that nurses and nuns would flock around her, more mesmerized than ever by her indomitable, charismatic presence. While personally I remember feeling sad and thinking how she had gone from accepting death to denying it.

The Denial of Death

Of all the patients who were interviewed in *On Death and Dying*, I do not remember a single person who did not believe in the afterlife. Yet rarely did they speak about what they thought lay in store for them. Although each of them (save for two holdouts) would come to accept that they were terminally ill—it was not the nature of the looming afterlife that obsessed them, it was the process of dying. What would it be like, what exactly did it mean? Paradoxically, it was their last remaining days on earth that would seem so much more precious to them than the spiritual eternity which was beckoning. Not surprisingly, those of her patients who did want to speak about the hereafter were conventional churchgoers, people who had spent most of their lives believing in God. They all seemed to say like a mantra, "I have no fear at all." They never mentioned purgatory or hell. They showed no hint of anxiety that their life was about to be judged. The attitude they embraced was one of calm submissiveness. God was calling them and they were now in his hands. "Thy will be done." It was as though God was going to take care of and solve any problem that might come up in the afterlife and what they had to do was get their final affairs in order on earth. Whatever thoughts they had of actually meeting God for the first time expressed a profound yearning to be cared for, loved and comforted. They did not seem to think God could be angry, critical of their conduct and certainly not punitive. They were mortally ill, at the end of their tether and it was not possible God would not feel sorry for them. As one seventeen-year-old girl who would soon die of a rare form of anemia—asked what she thought about dying—said, "It will be wonderful." Their sense of the hereafter was like that of a small child for whom there is no pain or worry that cannot immediately be assuaged by mommy or daddy. Their sense of eternity was that of peaceful, changeless contentment, the kind of imagined bliss that might precede your sweetest dream.

One of the most revealing of all Elizabeth Kübler-Ross's patients was Sister I, a young nun who had been rehospitalized with Hodgkin's disease and would soon die. A demanding, angry woman, disliked by the nursing staff when she joined the seminar, she would undergo a minor transformation at the hands of Elizabeth Kübler-Ross. For the first time in her life, she felt allowed to be herself, to be free to ventilate her hostility without being judged. Bolstered by such serendipitous relief, she was now able to show another side of herself—a loving, warm, affectionate side—she had not yet revealed. She told of her unexpected friendship with a Jewish man who was a patient across the hall. A jovial but unapologetic skeptic, he could hardly wait to inform Sister I that there really wasn't a God, that God was something people made up because they needed to. To her great surprise, she found that she enjoyed this challenge to her faith. Never before had she found it necessary to give reasons for her belief in God. Never before had she been stimulated to engage in such philosophical introspection. Because of it, in the final months of her life she became, in the touching words of Elizabeth Kübler-Ross, "what she wanted to be so badly, different from the others, yet still loved and accepted."

Sister I was unique among Elizabeth Kübler-Ross's patients, inasmuch as she combined conventional beliefs, personal vulnerability and very specialized religious training. She posed an even greater contrast when one compared her to the priests—who were neither patients nor chaplains in attendance at the seminar—but who served as the ordinary pastoral counselors to these unfortunate members of their flock in this time of their greatest need. They were the priests these dying patients went to in order to make their funeral arrangements; to stand in as crisis intervention counselors when necessary; and to comfort them in their final hours by perhaps reading their favorite Bible verse to them. They were the priests who—in stark contrast to Sister I—did not feel free to get in touch with their own vulnerability, their own doubts, their own resentment. Not surprisingly, all of these priests came across as holding fast to an infallible theology. The picture of their faith they wanted to present was one of unquestioning certainty. Within the structure of their authoritarian religion, there was no room for the admission of human fears. Although no doubt they felt considerable concern for these bereft, dying patients—some of whom they had known for many years—it seemed they could only relate in a distant and formal manner. As though doing the right thing, the politically correct thing, especially for a young priest, would be of far greater service as regards the ultimate fate of the dying patient's soul, than any mere expression of human empathy.

While reading *On Death and Dying*, I could not help but think of the patients I had known who had experienced, in one way or another, the process of dying. A crucial difference, of course, was that all of Elizabeth Kübler-Ross's patients—in spite of the fact they were almost always in deep denial—were in the very last stages of their illness with literally only days, weeks or months to live. These patients seemed eager to open up, perhaps because unconsciously they knew they would never get another chance. By contrast, the patients a therapist sees are rarely mortally ill when they begin therapy. I can think of only one patient in the past thirty years, who in the course of therapy with me would receive a diagnosis of terminal illness (a case that accordingly would affect me profoundly and that I would subsequently write about at great length in my first book, *The Portrait of the Artist as a Young Patient*). Typically, their initial encounter with the process of dying comes when a close family member or friend dies. Although there are vast differences in how people manage death, a universal reaction is shock. No matter how many times they have visited the person in the hospital, seen the signs of irreversible decline, and were advised the end was near, they are never prepared. The radical discontinuity between a person who is alive and one who is dead, between someone who has always existed and someone who has just stopped existing, is always, to a greater or lesser extent, traumatic. The denial that is so palpable in a patient who is dying—while, of course, not as overwhelming—is still quite powerful in the survivor who loved him.

Few deaths are as painful to bear as the death of a child. Here is Sybil, an hysterical, impulsive, elderly woman who has just lost her son:

> "You're sitting down, right? Good. Yesterday, Frank had a heart attack ... and ... HE DIED! Frank's DEAD! (cries uncontrollably) . . . He had just gone for a run on the beach ... he sat down on a bench, and he just keeled over. His friend who was with him tried to give him CPR, but it didn't work. He was dead by the time the paramedics got there."

Between long bouts of hysterical, angry weeping, I was able to gradually piece together what had happened. Frank, who had been living out of state for the past five years, had only six months ago returned to New York City. He had very much hoped to change his luck, to break the pattern of working at one dead-end sales job after another. And it was because he had just landed a promising new job that he had set off with a friend for a weekend of fun and games at Atlantic City. He had just turned forty-one. It was supposed to be a celebration! Over and over Sybil would say, as though of a miracle, "I just can't believe it;" as though the death of her son was without precedent in anything she had ever experienced or witnessed and certainly without any discernible cause. To help her make sense of what had happened, I asked if there had been any prior heart problems. "No." My question annoyed her, as if nothing could be less relevant at a time like this than mere facts. Yes, Frank had been overweight, had weighed 250 pounds, drank heavily, had some form of tuberculosis that was in latent form, and probably had not gone for a physical checkup in over fifteen years. Yet Sybil was adamant that that was no reason to get a heart attack.

The denial of death is reinforced by the complete absence of a transition between being alive and being dead. The impression is that of a person who has just inexplicably metamorphosed into his or her opposite (because all of the molecular and neurobiological changes leading to the climactic death have essentially been completely invisible to us).

In the following weeks, Sybil tried hard to blunt the edge of her hysterical grief by focusing on the funeral arrangements, or lack thereof. Barely able to subsist on her monthly social security check, she would discover just how expensive a funeral today could be. Cremation seemed the more economical way to go, but here too she could not afford the going rate. Desperate to honor her son's memory, as though Frank had always wanted nothing more than a proper burial, she decided to donate his body to science. She had been told, after removing the required donor organs, they would pay for the cremation of what remained. It would still not be enough because Sybil now wanted a plaque of some kind and a burial service in a decent cemetery to mark her son's passage. It didn't matter that it would wipe out the little savings she had. It didn't matter that Frank had been vociferously antireligious and would have been both outraged and guilt-stricken at the trouble his mother was going through. (He had once said to her, only half jokingly, "When I die, just dump my body in the nearest river.")

What did matter was that by going to such extremes Sybil could effectively take her mind off the profound panic about her own existence into which she had plunged. No detail of the impending funeral arrangement was therefore too small. She researched about half a dozen cemeteries in order to find one with just the right atmosphere. She spent hours writing and rewriting her son's epitaph, hoping she might capture in words the ineffable, tragic irony of having to attend her young son's funeral. She fretted about the excessive size of the urn of her son's ashes when she finally received it ("I guess it was so big because he weighed 250 pounds"). She contacted her former husband, who had been estranged from the family for the past twenty-five years, and graciously invited him to the services. (Afterwards Sybil would say, "His hand trembled when he shook my hand and all his hair was white.")

The obsessive attention to detail, or even the morbid lengths that patients such as Sybil will go to, is not uncommon. It is reminiscent in a curious way, or perhaps is the counterpart of that extraordinary hyper-vigilance expended—more often by prospective brides than husbands—on every aspect of an impending wedding. Rather than face the immense significance of culturally coded, deeply emotional, supposedly life-altering passages, patients typically would rather dwell on peripheral particulars.

Here is Roy, a thirty-two-year-old patient recently separated from his wife of the past ten years, and who—shortly after moving into the first furnished room he has ever lived in—has been shocked to learn that his best buddy since high school has unexpectedly died of a stroke.

> "I had come home late to find a note taped on my door. It was from Delores (his wife). It said, 'I am sorry to inform you that Chuck died yesterday morning from what they think is a stroke.'"
>
> "It was weird. Chuck had been very healthy, an athlete all his life. The week before he had experienced a terrible headache, and some dizziness while cleaning his yard, but he ignored it. Then, while cleaning the yard again, he just collapsed and was dead on arrival to the hospital.
>
> "I couldn't handle going to the funeral. What difference would it make if I did? Chuck wouldn't be there. But I wanted to go to the reception afterwards. We told Chuck stories, drank wine and toasted his memory. It didn't seem real that he had died. Somebody said jokingly, "You know,

if Chuck walked in here now, I don't
think any of us would be that surprised."

Roy tries to deal with the double depression of being separated
from his wife and the shock of losing his best friend by a half-
hearted attempt at gallows humor. Rather than going to the
funeral, he philosophizes about the mood of unreality and
dissociation that seems to hover over the reception. The ways
that patients such as Roy have of denying or forestalling having
to face the gravity and ultimate meaning of their own eventual
death, are myriad.

Hypochondriac concerns about the declining health of one's
aging parents is an unavoidable and almost universal
distraction. It is easier for David, a fifty-five-year-old, unmarried
man, to worry about his parents' ailments than to think about
the chronic loneliness that has driven him into treatment. He
says he accepts the fact that one day he will die, but he admits
he is not sure how well he will handle the death of his parents,
to whom he is deeply attached. He is all too eager, however, like
a surprising number of my patients, to discuss the supposedly
ambiguous conclusion of *The Sopranos* famous final episode.
"Tony got whacked. It's simple. Remember that flashback, with
him and Bobby in the boat? One of them wonders what it must
feel like to get hit and the other says, 'It's like going to black.'"

A longtime *Sopranos* fan, it is an offer I can't refuse, so I point
out there are other possibilities: such as the blackness standing
for the uncertainty and open-endedness of the future; or the
moral twilight into which each of the protagonists has
progressively descended; or the perpetual blank screen of our
experience which we as the viewer, and as every participant in
life, are obliged to fill in with the infinite variety of our
constructed meanings. When I soon realize David is more

willing to talk about Tony Soprano's fear of death than his own,
I switch gears. I ask if he ever wonders himself what the
experience of death must be like, which immediately prompts
the following conversation:

> "Do I think there's just blackness? No,
> I think there's something."
> "You mean an afterlife?"
> "Do I think someone is watching? No.
> Do I think, maybe like a chef, God, when
> He created the world, puts a little bit of
> this in and a little bit of that? ... I don't
> know."
> "He's just an observer then?"
> David laughs. "I don't know. I guess I'm
> on the fence when it comes to the
> afterlife."

In the protected space of a therapist's office, patients will often,
if given the chance, give voice to the vaguest of metaphysical
speculations. It is clear such rambling, ill-formed thoughts can
play little part in their real lives. But they do pay attention to
the brute fact of biological death, and the more they observe it
up close and personal, the more lasting its impact. Here is
Christopher, a very self-reflective New York artist, who has
returned from his father's funeral:

> "I was there when he died. We didn't
> talk, he had an oxygen mask on, but I
> spoke to him. I told him we had had some
> rough patches in our relationship when I
> was young, but we had managed to come

a long way since then. I said how much I admired the way he searched for personal meaning in his life and that he had never given up. I was holding his hand, and crying.

"I saw him die. It was strange. He just seemed to slip further and further from consciousness. The nurse came in and shined a light in his eyes. His pupils were frozen, dilated. I told her I didn't know what that meant and she said, 'He's actively dying now. Would you like me to give him a morphine drip? I said, I don't know, is he in pain? She said she couldn't tell for sure, she didn't think so, but sometimes it could facilitate the process of dying. Then don't do it, I said.

"I guess I wanted to just quietly be there when he died. He kept slipping away more and more. He didn't seem in pain. I saw it all. I saw the heart monitor stop, flatline, go beep and then hit zero. The end. And then there was this horrible startling death rattle, his lungs violently expelling the remaining breath in his body. It was the last sound or movement he would make. I looked at him, I knew he had just died and then he was just very still."

I asked Christopher, who over the years had often talked movingly about how troubling but meaningful his relationship with his father had been, if he was as relieved as he sounded. Yes, he said. It was a relief. It was peaceful. There was something reassuring about watching someone die. It seemed more natural.

Elizabeth Kübler-Ross is right when she says that people who work with the terminally ill soon lose their fear of death. The experience of calmly being with someone as they succumb to the final stage of life can be surprisingly demystifying, even uplifting. Watching the step-by-step way by which biological life support systems shut down, can put a naturalistic framework around a most primitive taboo. The impression of traumatic rupture, the sense that an invisible alien force has uncannily abducted a living soul, can now be supplanted by a more organic, comprehensibly causal perspective. Instead of being an enemy to life, death can be seen as a stopping point and this has been more or less the case for every patient who has observed someone die. As it was for James:

> "I was the only one who volunteered to stay in the hospice with her at the very end. I thought someone should be with my aunt. No matter how many hours it took, I was going to be there. And I was. Her breathing got more and more labored. She had been delirious for days, although occasionally she would call out my name. I put my hand on her forehead and whispered, 'Don't be afraid. It's all right. Let go, let go.' She couldn't hear me, but her breathing got fainter and fainter, and then, suddenly, she took a

tremendous gulp, and died." (James
cries.)

Where Elizabeth Kübler-Ross goes astray, however, is in the
way she seems to minimize the denial of death and to overvalue
the supposed final stage of acceptance. Although the anger and
depression triggered by a diagnosis of terminal illness are
significant, there is little doubt that the classic, unconscious
denial of death is the single most powerful (and usually
effective) defense mechanism. I don't think I have ever seen a
patient who fully overcame their denial of death, if only because
it is psychologically impossible to identify with the state of non-
existence. Admitting or believing one is going to die is not the
same thing as accepting it. To believe in the afterlife is to deny
the biological fact of death, if only because it implies the
continuation of consciousness or the soul in some form. And it
is a theme of this book, that it is extraordinarily difficult for
people to live their lives as they certainly would if they really
believed in the afterlife.

A final example of the power of denial. Jason is an assistant
principal, who was raised in a strict Catholic home and lives in
the shadow of his father whom he feels obliged to idealize. Here
is how he informed me, his father may be dying.

> Jason (smiling pleasantly): "Well, dad's
> not doing well."
> Me: "The operation wasn't successful?"
> Jason: "They found a tumor in his
> colon."
> Me: "Was it malignant?"
> Jason: "Cancer."

Me: "I'm sure you're concerned, even though you seem calm."

Jason: "I am not. No point in worrying about what you can't control."

Me: "Was it early detection? Do you know the prognosis?"

Jason (shrugging): "Don't really know. Dad doesn't like to talk about these things. We don't usually get into vulnerable feelings. He's very religious."

Me: "And you?"

Jason (pause): "Yeah, I guess I go along. I don't pray for an intervention and neither does Dad. But he says he likes it when other people pray for him."

James smiles briefly. He has been well schooled to face every adversity with as much dignity as possible, to never let them see you sweat. He reveals his father has been diagnosed with cancer, the extent of which is unknown, but he denies he is concerned about his father's fate. He points out that his father also does not like to talk about those kinds of things, and he matter-of-factly adds—"We don't usually get into vulnerable feelings"—as though this refusal was purely a matter of personal choice. He drives the point home, and probably in his own mind says all there is to say by commenting that his father is "very religious." When attempting to make the conversation more personal and less socially correct, I ask—"And you?"—he begins to founder. He concedes he is religious in the sense of trying to live up to parental expectations, but he hints at heterodox tendencies such as not particularly believing in the power of prayer. However, lest we get the wrong idea, he hurries to add that his dad also does not pray for a miracle. He humorously notes, however, that his dad likes it when other people pray for him, thereby ending the conversation the same way it began—on a pleasant social note.

From this small extract, we can see how Jason lives his life within the safe circle of his defenses. The more highly charged the event, the more we are defended. And when faced with the death of our father, no defense is more potent than denial.

Sherwin Nuland is a world famous surgeon, who has written brilliantly and passionately from a medical perspective what Elizabeth Kübler-Ross has covered so masterfully from a psychological standpoint. His book, *How We Die*, was an almost instant classic. Like Elizabeth Kübler-Ross, Sherwin Nuland believes that the more patients learn about how the body dies, the less they are terrified of death. Unlike Elizabeth Kübler-Ross, however, he believes that "when you're dead, you're dead." The out-of-body and near-death experiences that so impressed Elizabeth Kübler-Ross, he explains by pointing to the varying physiological reactions dying people undergo vis-à-vis the loss of oxygen to the brain: some hallucinate and some, due to a sudden endorphin rush, experience a not uncomfortable numbing defense. (As a striking example of the latter, Nuland reports that once, while drowning with his backpack on, feeling strangely calm, he thought, "I'm going to drown right here in a pool in front of everyone—isn't that absurd!.")

In a sense I think that Elizabeth Kübler-Ross and Sherwin Nuland are both right and both wrong. They are right that learning about the processes of dying and observing it up to a point, have a calming effect. They are wrong to think that the amount of exposure to the process of dying can be almost limitless. As wonderful as *How We Die* is, there are few who do not find the act of reading it—not to speak of the actual experience of being there and witnessing what he writes about so graphically—harrowing. They do not realize that the classic denial of death that lies deep in the unconscious might work considerably better up until the experience of actually beginning the death process. It may be true at that desperate point that we would most likely be more prepared had we read Nuland's book, or observed first hand, as Christopher and James did, the life support system of a dying person shut down one by one. It is wrong to suppose such exposure has no boundaries and carries no liabilities. Indeed, the hypochondriacal reaction to the prospect of death, so common in patients such as David, often has its roots in the detached and morbid observation of the inevitable decline of one's erstwhile insuperable parents. And accordingly there are few patients who can tolerate witnessing the actual death of their parents for more than just a very short time without being irreversibly scarred by the experience (psychodynamically, what happens is that when such morbid memories pass a certain threshold, the person cannot help but internalize them to an unhealthy degree).

Let me close with an animal analogue. The great evolutionary biologist, W.D. Hamilton, once conjectured that the way in which a captured, struggling prey, in its final death throes, at last seems to submit to its fate—may be a biological adaptation in which the life-preserving pain-feedback mechanisms suddenly switch off (there no longer being a point to feeling pain). And if you are a fan of the great nature documentaries (as I am) televised regularly on *Animal Planet* and *National Geographic*, that is just what you see. Inevitably, there comes a point when the brave but doomed water buffalo seems to give up and allow the lion to pull him to its certain death or when the terrified impala stops trying to squirm free from the killing-machine jaws of the leopard and seems to choose to become still.

Analogously, it may be that nature protects us from being overly terrified of our inevitable death right up to the moment of our death throes. At which point, the denial of death is switched off and a strange, endorphin-charged, body-numbing, seeming acceptance of the death process takes over: i.e., Sherwin Nuland's tranquil reflection that he was about to drown in a pool, with everyone watching.

In other words, it may be that if we tinker too much with the exquisite balance between the denial of death and the final acceptance of death—we do so at our peril. It may be the reason Elizabeth Kübler-Ross at the end of her life seemed to lose her way in a sea of mystical ideas. It may be that she insisted far too much on exposing her unconscious to a superhumanly abnormal degree of traumatic exposure to contact with the processes of death and dying.

CHAPTER FOUR

PATIENTS TALK ABOUT THE AFTERLIFE

"And I am angry at God."

This is Olivia, the feisty, fiftyish, Irish mother who refuses to accept the loss of her son on September 11, 2001.

"It was like him to go back and try to
help the others."

It was stupid to think of the others when he could have saved himself. It was stupid of the government not to have seen the warning signs, and it was infuriating to then try to cover up their mistakes with lies. It had never occurred to me the amiably chatty receptionist of the doctor I had been routinely seeing at the time of the catastrophe could be so directly involved. Hours after the morning of September 11, and throughout that traumatic first week, I had seen most of my patients and listened to their sometimes surreal stories. The man sitting at the outdoor cafe puzzling over the thousands of pigeons which had abruptly taken flight from the roof of the Twin Towers; who had watched fascinated but uncomprehendingly at first one and then a second plane fly into a tower, when it dawned on him that he had to find and save his wife from a terrifying attack. The woman who had seen people, the size of specks, jumping together to their certain deaths from the now scalding hot rooftops. And, perhaps most memorably, the man whose vacationing friends—upon returning to their nearby penthouse apartment—would discover two airplane seats with their corpses still strapped in them, sprawled in the middle of their living room (having been shot like missiles from an exploding plane straight through their ceiling).

But no one I knew had suffered the kind of loss Olivia had. No one had experienced the post-traumatic stress she had endured. She had gone for three visits to the counselor they had offered her and then quit.

> "There's nothing anybody can say that
> will change things. I can go to a priest,
> but I don't want to."

She would rather stay busy than talk. She does not see herself letting go of her anger. "I will never understand it. Maybe, one day when I die, it will be explained to me." She is angry at God but she does not doubt that there is a God, and she does not doubt that God, if He wanted to, could explain it to her. Olivia, like Sybil, cannot accept the cruel death of her son, and bitterly calls upon God for an answer. Unconsciously, she knows she is looking for something she cannot find: a satisfying explanation for how a loving God could stand by while her son was being burned to a crisp. Her reaction was not uncommon. Those who directly lost family members as a result of the September 11 attack—and the more religious they were, the more this was so—have to struggle to be consoled by their faith. While the reverse was true for those lucky ones who managed to get out alive: it was proof there was a God, that God was merciful, if ever one was needed. The contradiction between God as a good shepherd leading his flock out of the jaws of a fiery inferno and a God who silently and passively watches his flock being consumed was hardly noted.

Eileen is a prototypical New York artist. She grew up in a suburban small town, got a fine arts degree, moved to Manhattan, supported herself with a series of somewhat degrading, menial part-time jobs and began painting in earnest. Her one goal was to do beautiful work, not to become famous and successful. Although she is intellectually against organized religion, having long since left the church she was brought up in, she considers herself an intensely spiritual person. When, shortly after coming to New York, she encountered her first homeless couple sleeping under some filthy blankets, she invited them to come live with her. For two weeks they stayed together as a family in her one-room studio apartment until they were ready to leave. She was puzzled when I tried to point out to her how strangely self-sacrificial her offer had been. She did not consider herself a Christ-like person, she was just someone who put compassion above all other human values. Not surprisingly, at the height of the AIDS epidemic in the '80's, she was the one whom her dying gay friends would seek out for special care: to change their dressings, wash their bodies, bring them food and sit with them.

Her first impulse on the afternoon of September 11 had been to give blood, but she was too frail and anemic for that. So she volunteered for whatever she could. She helped distribute the famous, haunting posters of missing persons—"Have you seen _____?"—that began cropping up spontaneously all over the city. When it was reopened to the public, she began regularly visiting Ground Zero. She took it upon herself to personally let the men in the local firehouse know how much she appreciated their heroic rescue efforts on September 11. She became

enraged at her fellow New Yorkers who complained about the
heightened security measures, who calibrated the impact of
September 11 mainly in terms of the disruptions it caused in
their personal lives: "I hate these people on the Lower East Side
who walk around with breathing masks on. As though to say,
I'm smarter than you. I'm protecting myself from possible toxic
air pollution."

Two years before September 11, Eileen's younger sister had
been instantly killed by a drunken driver who had blindsided
her car. Her furious message to me on my answering machine
had been an anguished "MY SISTER'S DEAD." But I knew it
was a loss she was unlikely to recover from, that the clinical
depression that had driven her to therapy in the first place
would only deepen. And for about a year thereafter she suffered
from recurring, terrifyingly real nightmares, typically in which
she was wildly tunneling under the ground, trying desperately
to escape from something terrible that was chasing her. Against
my advice, she began upping the dosage of the anti-anxiety
medication upon which she relied. She blamed herself for not
having died in her sister's stead, for senselessly being allowed
to continue her own useless life. Over and over, she tried to
memorialize her sister's death by drawing—first one, then
another, then hundreds and hundreds of symbolic images—of
the car she had been innocently sitting in when the fatal
accident had occurred. She became fascinated with the menace
that lurked beneath the surface of things, the underbelly of life:
rats that lived in the walls; worms that thrived in the intestinal
tract; creepy ideas that might spring anytime from the
unconscious. It was her duty as an artist to explore and capture
in her work this seething, dark side, the nihilistic randomness
of the world that in a single instant could snuff out the shining
presence of someone like her sister. By directing her bitterness

towards the world's hypocrisy, she managed to hold on to her fragile spiritualism.

Although she scoffed at the idea of heaven or hell, she believed there was "something else" beyond the grave besides the physical. She didn't know what or where this was. She didn't know if her sister's consciousness survived, if she continued to have feelings, if she was happy. She wanted to, but could not sense her sister's presence. She would have loved for her sister to figure out some way to contact her from the other side, but she never did. She had no expectations of meeting up with her sister, after she herself died. All she could say was that her sister's spirit was "out there" and that if it did not, could not communicate with her she at least could speak to it. When I asked Eileen what she had meant by that, she said, "Well, if I have a certain thought . . . like 'can this rotten world get any more horrible than it is?' . . . I just say it out loud, and the fact that she *might* hear it comforts me."

Although she lived an unconventional life, Eileen's picture of the afterlife, and the relationship to it that she has, is a familiar one. On the one hand, she is deeply curious about the possibility of her sister's posthumous existence; on the other, her thoughts about it could not be more scattered, amorphous and transient. She only knows she feels better if she sometimes gives voice to what is weighing on her mind, in the imagined presence of her idealized dead sister.

Patients are like that. In the immediate wake of a particularly unbearable loss, they will often address the person who has just died. They do not expect to be heard, but find it soothing to talk to the other as though they were still alive. To understand this, think of an incident that still rankles in the memory: a person perhaps upon whom you set great store, who for no apparent reason walked out on you. Someone remembering that, and still feeling the old resentment, might then say aloud, to himself, "You shouldn't have done that." It may not make sense, but it feels good. In effect they say to the substitutive memory what they did not get a chance to say in real life.

This is what Christopher (from the last chapter), shortly after his father had died, had wanted to do. As he put it:

> "I don't know why. I tried to have an
> imaginary conversation in my mind with
> my dad . . . I was wondering if it might
> make me feel better, but it didn't."

Sometimes patients, even many years after a parent has died, will address him or her, usually in a very simple, affectionate way: "You know, Dad, I wish you were here."

After a long and unhappy marriage to a withdrawn alcoholic, Jenny had been delighted to finally meet a man whom she considered surprisingly loving and responsive. Soon after she decided to remarry, she invited her new husband to accompany her in a visit to her father's grave. It had been years since she had traveled to the out of the way cemetery in Brooklyn, and she could barely remember where the inexpensive family plot was. But now she had a special purpose. Finding her father's headstone at last, she approached it alone, her husband respectfully standing behind. Getting on her hands and knees, she kissed the flat stone and then asked her husband to join her. Standing up and gesturing, as though introducing one person to another at a social function, Jenny said: "Dad, I want to introduce you to Leonard. He's my husband. I love him very much. I know you would have liked him. Here he is (beckoning to her husband to come forward)."

When I discussed this afterwards with Jenny, she was clear about what she didn't believe in. She didn't believe in heaven or hell. She didn't think her father could actually hear what she was saying. She didn't know where he was or if he was any place. She did think there might be something after death. Hadn't she heard that atoms are immortal? That they may break apart, but can't be destroyed? So why couldn't the human body, after it decomposed, recompose itself in some new way that would allow consciousness to continue? She therefore believes, like Eileen, there is "something" after death and she knows she somehow feels closer to her father's spirit after she talks to it.

Of course, patients pray to God, and depending on how religious they are, they will sometimes speak to God. They almost never wish for God to speak to them. Here is John, a lapsed Catholic, who nevertheless continues to believe in his Savior, telling me about a very disturbing encounter with his best friend:

> "I thought I knew Stan, but I guess I don't. We were talking about why we had gone to the colleges we went to, when, out of the blue he said, 'God told me to go to college.' I thought he was joking, but he wasn't. It gave me a very weird feeling. I believe in God, but I certainly don't believe in visions or voices from above. People who say they have those kinds of experiences strike me as nuts. So I began pressing Stan to see just how serious he was. I said how can you possibly be sure that a voice, any voice you hear, can be that of God?

"Very calmly, Stan countered my
objections. 'Look,' he said, 'imagine
you're in this room by yourself, and clear
as a bell, you hear a voice informing you
it is God, and it tells you, you have to go
to college. Now wouldn't you believe it?'

"Something about the quiet, confident
way Stan said this, made me try to
imagine being in such a situation, and
suddenly I wasn't so sure anymore."

John stopped and waited for my clinical diagnosis, which
meant he wanted me to tell him whether his best friend was
secretly psychotic or not. When I told him I didn't know Stan
well enough to make that judgment, he immediately asked how
many of my patients, statistically speaking, have claimed to
have heard the voice of God? When I said I didn't have those
figures handy off the top of my head, he inquired as to my
general position on the subject of hallucinations and visions.
What exactly were my views, anyway? It was only when I then
pointed out—because he did not like my answers—he seemed
to be pressing me in much the same way he had pressed Stan,
that John calmed down and for the first time reflected on his
familiar argumentative streak. In the past, we had worked on
how, whenever he was frightened or unsure of himself, he
tended to lash out at others. Suddenly, he remembered what he
considered a significant incident from his college days.

"I knew this guy, I think he might have
been Greek Orthodox, I don't know, but
he was very, very mystical and he
worshipped Christ. He made me uneasy,

but you couldn't forget him. He had this way of explaining anything that happened, of interpreting it, by referring to a particular parable in the New Testament that, to him, held the key. I had never known anyone who did that. I didn't know why, but it bothered me. Maybe it has something to do with why I rarely go to church.

"Anyway, this guy, I don't remember his name, had been in the same philosophy class at City College with Stan and me. At the beginning of the semester, he had loudly proclaimed in the hallway, for anyone who cared to listen, that if it turned out this teacher was a 'dirty, rotten atheist' as others had been, he would drop the course. So far he had managed to stick it out, until the day came we were told that no less a celebrity than the notorious and controversial Ayn Rand, author of *Atlas Shrugged*, a radical, libertarian, anti-liberal would be visiting our philosophy department.

"Because of who she was, her lecture was moved to the main auditorium and it was jam packed. I sat with Stan, and next to him was this guy, who seemed to get along with Stan. I don't know if you've seen Ayn Rand, but she's a trip. She's a big and bold woman, speaks with an accent and acts like she's infallible. She

wears a pin in the shape of a dollar sign,
to pay homage to the power of capitalism.
She despises the welfare state, everything
it stands for, and thinks liberals are
spineless worms. I'd say over 90% of the
students at City College were probably
liberals at that time.

"Ayn Rand is a hardcore atheist who
calls her philosophy Objectivism. People
who believe in God are mental cowards
who cannot face the obvious truth. We
live in a society that has carried relativism
to a point of sickness, that no longer
believes in the absolute values of good and
evil, that sees only grays, that has lost its
compass. Once in a television interview,
when asked about her ideas, she stated
that she considered herself the greatest
philosopher since Aristotle.

"She was so over the top, so different
from what I was used to hearing, that I
admit I found her oddly stimulating. One
of her main ideas, that selfishness could
be positive, that we had been too
brainwashed by the Christian ethos of
self-sacrifice, anticipated by decades
Gordon Gekko's famous credo—'Greed is
Good'—in Oliver Stone's *Wall Street*.

"The entire audience had listened in a
very subdued way and I couldn't tell what
kind of impact she had made, or if she had
had any impact at all. At the end, she

volunteered to answer questions. The first
hand up was from my mystical friend. He
did not hesitate to stand up when he was
picked and to my surprise he had no
problem in projecting his normally soft
voice across much of the auditorium to
the podium.

"I dreaded what might be coming and
tried to hide my face in anticipation of an
embarrassing confrontation. But what he
did was quite clever. Concealing the
punch line until the very end, he began
calmly by philosophically and concisely
summarizing his key ideas. Then, noting
that in her entire system there was no
place for the universal and indispensable
value of Christian love—his voice
suddenly and dramatically rising—he
concluded, 'So I say, that I find your
philosophy at bottom to be hollow and
rotten!'

"And Ayn Rand just exploded, I mean
she went berserk. 'GET OUT . . . GET
OUT . . . I DON'T DEBATE WITH
RELIGIOUS FANATICS.' She was
screaming and waving her arms furiously.
Apparently the auditorium was not a big
enough place for both of them. Either the
mystic was going to leave or she would
walk off the stage. So, obviously pleased
with having done what he must have

thought was the Lord's work, he quietly and with a lot of dignity walked out.

"The next day, however, along with Stan, I was summoned to the assistant Dean's office, where the mystic was already waiting. Word had gotten out we were his friends, so we had been called as witnesses or co-defendants to the incident that had occurred. I could see that he was agitated, with none of the bravura he had displayed in standing up to Ayn Rand. Stan spoke first, then I followed. I patterned what I said after Stan, doing my best to put a good face on what had happened.

"What I'll always remember is what the mystic did, when it was his turn. I had expected at least a little bit of fire and brimstone, but he was trembling and staring off into space. 'Sir,' he began, plaintively, 'when Christ drove out the money changers from the temple . . .'

"He got no further than that. 'Now, son,' interrupted the Dean, bending over backwards to be a just arbiter, 'this is not the place for that.' That is all it took. One simple take-charge gesture and the spiritual frenzy into which he had worked himself utterly collapsed."

Initially cowed by his friend's spiritual fervor, John had felt vicariously vindicated by the unexpected turnabout. It served to fortify his belief that a person's religious views should never be made public. What could it accomplish to tell someone you saw a vision, or heard a voice? He had been upset by both Stan and the mystic, because each of them had crossed the line between the practical, mundane world we are all forced to live in, and the very personal, private, spiritual realm that is ours alone. When I asked John what his own personal view of the afterlife was, he quickly replied:

> "I believe in Christ. I have no idea what
> the afterlife is like, and I don't see any
> point in thinking about it. I'll find out
> soon enough. Meanwhile I try to live a
> decent life and hope for the best."

Like so many others, John uses religion as a kind of spiritual comforter, to be put away and saved for a rainy day. He has no use for the rituals and trappings of organized religion, which seem to him an impractical waste of time. He does not think religion should be taken seriously, views it as one more support system and is threatened by religious zealots like his former college friend and—if he really is one—his current best friend, Stan.

Very different from John, it is the spiritual poverty, the dismal unfeeling indifference of the world she lives in that so threatens Stephanie. It would have been nice if religions were true, but ever since she was a teenager it was obvious to her that the stories in the Bible were "patently absurd" fairy tales. Raised in a secular household, it had been left up to her to make what she could of the afterlife. And it had never been a question that interested her. Death was the end, the last exit, it was where everything stopped. Why look beyond—at nothingness? Life was what interested her. It was her only hope.

And for Stephanie, hope was what the sixties were all about. Bob Dylan, Abbie Hoffman, the Mamas and the Papas, Woodstock. They all meant hope. As a teenager she would travel to Manhattan to go to the Village Gate, sip a vodka Gibson and feel very cool herself as she listened to the latest and baddest in contemporary jazz. She felt especially prepared, far more sophisticated than her classmates when she entered City College as a freshman. She was unafraid to ride the underground subway trains, and actually enjoyed walking through Harlem. Hope.

That was then and this was now when she first came to see me. Along with the passage of time, there had been the waning of her marriage, the fading of her early beauty, the curse of menopause and the pernicious inroads of the aging process.

"I guess I'm beginning to realize that I'm going to be leaving this earth one day," she had said wistfully shortly after meeting me. Nothing had turned out the way she had wanted. If her greatest disappointment, her biggest loss had been the loss of hope, she would nevertheless cling doggedly to life. If no one would care for her, she would doctor herself. She was a fan of Gary Null, the nutritional guru, and she herself was a crackerjack when it came to the right vitamins, the proper organic diet, and the most holistic, preventive medicine. But much as she favored alternative medicine, she was not shy— once she spotted the faintest possible abnormality—about running to her internist, her orthopedist, her ophthalmologist and her dermatologist. Going to the doctor was sheer agony for her but it was worse not to go. To protect herself against disappointment, she would automatically imagine the worst. When her ophthalmologist detected a very, very slowly growing cataract in her right eye that might or might not, many years from now, require surgery—by the way "one of the safest operations currently being done," he assured her—she immediately told herself, "I'll probably lose an eye." When she fell on her left knee and tore a ligament that required a dozen strenuous sessions with a physical therapist, she said, "I don't think my knee will ever stop hurting me."

When I pointed out for someone so cynical about life, she seemed to be dearly holding on to it, she immediately quipped, "What's the alternative?"

I never could get Stephanie to talk about the alternative. Death meant extinction. The mother of all losses. To think about the afterlife was like thinking about a black hole. It frightened her too much. But she was more than willing to talk about the death of a young orthodox rabbi she had observed and experienced as an eighteen-year-old Red Cross volunteer, at a time when her hope was in full bloom.

> "He was twenty-five, with terminal brain cancer. I was supposed to visit him five days a week, for about three months up until the time he died. He was very nice. I think he liked my coming, sitting with him and just talking. He seemed interested in my life, he would ask questions about what I was doing. I was told not to talk about his medical condition and he never mentioned his sickness. He didn't talk about his feelings, but he didn't seem frightened either. He seemed sad. He was quiet and sometimes he would even laugh at one of my jokes.

"His family visited him a lot. His mother, his relatives, I think they appreciated the fact I was coming to see him, but they never spoke to me. They would huddle around the bed, and sometimes they would draw the curtain around the bedside.

"I guess I got attached to him, so I felt really bad when he died. He was very religious and I think that was his consolation, his answer for any questions he might have had about the afterlife."

When she had hope, she did not have the need to obsess about her own death. She could calmly observe and participate in an obviously meaningful way with a dying rabbi. She could nostalgically evoke the tender bond that had sprung up between them. It was only when her own hope, her basic trust in the goodness of life began to fail her, that the grinning skull of her eventual death began to mock her. Stephanie is just one of many patients who view the afterlife as a kind of bitter black hole, the thought of which alternately sickens and terrifies them. It is perhaps the antithesis of the Norman Rockwell picture-perfect Heaven, the consoling dream, the long-anticipated reward for so many of Elizabeth Kübler-Ross' dying patients; for fanatical, born-again Christians like Sonny Dewey; for joyful evangelists eagerly awaiting the rapture, like my cleaning lady.

Patients in short have various attitudes towards the promise of a spiritual afterlife. There is hope. There is doubt. There is joy. There is fear. And then—when the blows one is asked to endure become Job-like and unbearable—there is rage. Marshall is a successful financial analyst who prides himself on being a no-

nonsense skeptic concerning all things supernatural. In his mid-thirties, he comes across as being well-defended, in charge of himself, accepting of the fact that the life we have here is all there is, but it wasn't always this way. He can still remember as though it was yesterday his tortured adolescence, the household crises that, one after another, kept coming and seemed like they would never end, and the twenty years it would take him to realize his own mother had been insane.

"A year before I started seeing you, shortly before my mother died, there had been this other psychiatrist. I had been talking about visiting my mother in her condominium in Miami, and the letter she had sent me afterwards. For some reason he wanted to see it, so I brought it to him the next session. He read it slowly, as though he were examining it. Then he looked right at me . . . he didn't have what you'd call the greatest bedside manner . . . and he said, 'Your mother is insane.'

"It just went through me. Not once in my life had I considered even the possibility. Sure my mother was hysterical, she was deeply unhappy, she could lose all control. I could accept that. As my father would say . . . who was her doormat . . . whenever I would ask him why he put up with everything he put up with, 'You know your mother; what can I do?'

"You're probably going to ask me why the psychiatrist thought my mother was insane from just one letter. Or maybe you already know. Well, he pointed to the tiny writing all along the margins. The microscopic attention to the most trivial details. The bizarre ideas. It was more than a thought disorder, he said. It was paranoid ideation."

One simple sentence had electrified Marshall, had upended the safe house he had created for himself, and rewritten the history of his family's dynamics. The suffering he had endured had not been just the understandable aftermath of a desperately unhappy woman who could not control herself. His mother had not just been the wounded and maddened victim of an uncaring, hostile world. Suddenly, with his new insight, he could make sense of things that had always baffled him. Why, for example, his mother had seemed to hate sex. Why she would say over and over that a man who had sex with a woman before he was married was a 'bum.' That the very act of intercourse, 'a man going into a woman,' gave her the creeps. That, even worse than that, was for someone to marry outside of their religion, which was 'evil.' For Marshall's mother, who was Jewish, that meant marrying a Christian. But most of all, he could understand in a new light the two darkest years of his life.

"We had moved from Seattle to New York when I was fifteen. I think my mother had wanted to keep an eye on my older sister, Cora, who was a sophomore at Columbia University.

"Terrible stories had been steadily coming back to her from Esther, her sister, with whom Cora had been staying. Something strange was going on. Cora had stopped coming home at night, sometimes for days at a time. Was she on drugs? Was she under someone's spell?

"My mother would find out. She had to know. At the very least she would see to it that Cora came home each and every night. Not once could I remember my sister ever standing up to my mother and defying her. But that was two years ago, when Cora, still living with us, had been sixteen. Esther was right. Something had really changed. At eighteen, she was bigger, stronger looking, more full-bodied, more womanly looking. She had always been stubborn and proud, but now she was defiantly so. No, she was not doing drugs. No, she was not seeing anyone. She was simply staying with her friends. She was enjoying her independence. She was eighteen now and it was her right to make her own decisions.

"What had worked in Seattle, did not work in the Lower East Side. When my mother tried to physically stop my sister from going out at night, by barring the door, she found herself easily and firmly moved to one side. For the first time, instead of the untamable driving force behind our household, I saw my mother as weak and pathetic.

"Unable to control my sister, so far as her comings and goings went, my mother took to spying on her. She recruited Esther as her lookout, and together they began hanging around the Columbia University campus in the hope of catching my sister in the act. Whatever Cora was doing, my mother was certain it had to be evil.

"Then one afternoon Esther, looking very worried, took me aside. My mother was beginning to frighten her. She was having these outbursts, these fits of screaming right in the middle of a crowded subway car. They would be coming home together after another fruitless attempt to catch even a glimpse of my elusive sister in the labyrinthine byways of Columbia University. Suddenly, my mother would clasp her hands together, and looking upward, in a keening, anguished voice, repeat, "MOMMY . . . MOMMY . . . MY DAUGHTER IS A WHORE. . ." over and over again.

"I didn't know how much more of this I could take, and I couldn't wait for my sister to leave. So I thought I would be glad when the day came when Cora popped in, empty carton in hand, and tersely announced she was moving out. But when I looked at my mother, my heart sank. In all her fits and rages, I had never seen her seem so crushed, so defeated. As a last stand, she planted her back against the door and dug in her heels. She was barely over five feet tall and didn't weigh much more than a hundred pounds. She moaned, "Good Jewish girls don't leave home before they're married." Cora, carton of clothes in one hand, began slowly and stubbornly pulling my mother away from the door with the other. Sensing that the end of something had arrived, my mother issued her final ultimatum: 'If you walk out that door, you can never come back.' Then my mother, exhausted, kind of slid to the floor as my sister angrily wedged the door open just enough to squeeze through and make her departure.

"I'll always remember my mother sitting on the floor crying. You know those homeless, down and out people you see sitting on the sidewalks staring into space? My mother reminded me then of one of them. It took ten years for me to even think of forgiving Cora for the pain she had caused.

"It was better with Cora gone, for everyone, but there was still one more horrible day to go. It was my father's turn to take me aside to whisper the startling, terrifying news. Cora was married! She was pregnant! But her husband was NOT JEWISH! He was the son of a prominent Dutch brain surgeon.

"I don't know who was more scared, my father or myself as we waited to see what my mother's reaction was going to be. She seemed momentarily relieved to hear her daughter was married, perhaps an honest woman at last, though dismayed to hear she was already pregnant and not knowing what that meant, but she was visibly stricken at the words *not Jewish*: 'Cora married a goy. MOMMY . . . MOMMY.' Then she stopped, suddenly enraged, looked up, and started shaking her fist: 'YOU BASTARD, GOD! YOU'RE A SON OF A BITCH . . . I'VE BEEN A GOOD JEW ALL MY LIFE . . . AND YOU DO THIS TO ME . . . YOU ROTTEN BASTARD!'

"It was almost comical. My father wanted to be the mediator between God and my mother . . . two equally matched opponents in his eyes . . . but he didn't know how. And I, who wasn't much of a believer at that time, found myself thankful there had not been immediate payback from above."

The revelation, and now belief, that his mother all along was clinically insane comes as a release and relief for Marshall. The implacable influence she had continued to exercise over his life, his choices, in spite of all his efforts to establish his independence, now seemed weakened. If the indomitable woman who had shaken her fist at God had been mad, if she had been out of touch with reality rather than fearless, then Marshall might find a long sought after liberation. In his own subtle way, he had been as defiant of his mother as Cora had been, save for the fireworks. He had fashioned a life as different from his mother's as Cora's, but he had made every major decision with his mother as the reference point. If hardly a dialogue, his life had been one long debate with the spirit of his mother. Now he could begin to search for meaning against an entirely new reference point: his own true self. And with personal liberation came at least partial forgiveness. No longer did he feel the need to be condescending to his mother, to see her either as a devouring force or a tormented, crushed spirit. He could begin to see her for the sick, suffering, lost soul that she was. Now, whenever he evoked her memory, as he often did, and talked to it, as he often did, he could say, with genuine sympathy:

> "Mom, I wish I could understand what happened to you to make you the way you were. I wish I could have helped you more, but I couldn't."

Timothy, a tall, dashing, transplanted Englishman, is an indispensable, all-purpose creative director at a leading New York advertising agency. He is the go-to person when they need someone to make a smashing presentation to a hot new prospect. He is the deep thinker they call upon when they want someone to meticulously map out a long-term product strategy. He is the analyst they turn to when a brand identity mysteriously begins to lose its seductive flavor.

But Timothy is also the person they choose when it comes to pro bono work. They know that the greater the cause, the more humanitarian the project, the more his finely-honed liberal values will rise to the challenge. And on this particular occasion, Timothy could hardly wait to tell me about it:

> "The idea was originally that of an eccentric multi-millionaire venture capitalist. He had heard that the number one request of dying children was to go to Disneyland and see Mickey, so he decided to build a special Disneyland camp just for kids who had cancer. For an entire week, at no expense, they could relax, have fun and see their beloved Mickey and Disneyland to their heart's content.
>
> "The purpose of the ad I was shooting was to promote this camp and the work it was doing. It is already pretty famous, but the founder wasn't satisfied; he felt it deserved to be much more widely known.
>
> "That was my job and of course, a successful pro bono campaign could only make the agency look good."

It was obvious, in the course of directing the shoot, that Timothy had been deeply affected by what he had seen.

"The children are selected from poor families, based on the letters they or their parents send to Mickey. It's amazing, isn't it, that by far the number one request of dying children is to see Mickey Mouse? Says something about America, doesn't it?

"Well, these kids range from seven or eight to twelve, thirteen years old. They all have advanced cancer. The camp has a full medical staff, and some of these kids, you should see them, they get all kinds of shots every day and sometimes are all hooked up to machines.

"The star of the commercial was Sean, a ten-year-old boy. He had no hair, he was tall for his age and amazingly thin, but he did all the activities and he really liked to swim. So the commercial, it's 30 seconds, follows him around. It ends with a shot of Sean, you see him underneath the water, swimming towards the surface. There's this incredible, joyful smile as his head crashes through the surface and his arms fly up.

"The last line is, 'My name is Sean. If you have cancer, like me, you can come to Disneyland Camp, too.'"

I asked Timothy, since he had not only created and directed the campaign but written the copy, too, how Sean had felt about saying the word cancer aloud.

Surprisingly, he did not seem to have considered the question before:

> "Well . . . he did have trouble saying it. I guess, as obvious as it must be that they are terribly sick, they don't like to think about what having cancer really means. I had to make him say it, though, it was the point of the whole campaign."

Two weeks later Timothy arrived for the session looking glum and soulful. An unexpected letter he had received from Sean's father, which he asked to read to me, had thrown him into a pensive mood:

> "I want to tell you how much Marge (his mother) and me appreciate everything you did for Sean at Disneyland Camp. We were afraid he might overexert himself when he first went down there, but he didn't. He was surprisingly lively when he came home. For about a week, he talked about nothing else but Disneyland Camp. He had never liked the water and never thought he would go in the pool, so he was really proud of the way he swam. He just couldn't get over that shot of him bursting up through the water and smiling. He showed that video you gave him to all his friends and must have

watched it by himself in his room about twenty times.

"I'm writing this so you will know just how happy you made Sean. Marge and I would have liked to have gone down there and thanked you in person. But as you know, we have no money.

"Well, Sean died last Tuesday. The funeral was Friday . . ."

Unable to continue, Timothy breaks down and weeps uncontrollably. In the five years I have known him, it is by far the most emotional I have seen him. A brilliant, caustic intellectual, he can be unforgiving when it comes to dissecting the layered hypocrisies of American and British culture, especially when it comes to organized religion. He is proud of the early education he has given his two teenage daughters on the massive contradictions that underlie the historical rise of the Judaic-Christian religion. When asked about the afterlife, which he almost never thinks about, he concedes there may be "something" after death, but he doesn't know what.

Like so many patients, Timothy is caught completely off guard and swept away by the terrible moment, the traumatic discontinuity and unimaginable lacuna when life ends and death begins. There is at that moment, which of course comes differently for different people, a kind of double sadness. The sadness of the person who has just died, with whom one now passionately identifies, who has just lost everything in the world they ever treasured in one fell swoop, and the sadness of the suddenly solitary survivor who now has to reframe, rethink and revise every single thought, feeling and association he ever had or will have concerning the freshly dead, vanished other.

We can see this is no easy task, as Freud famously noted in his classic *Mourning and Melancholia*. One solution is to cultivate dead memories rather than dead persons: it being far less stressful to think of the presently dead other as they used to be rather than as they are not only now but for all time. It is understandable, yet remarkable when you think about it, how unwilling people are to reflect upon the likely existential status—whether one of posthumous, transcendental continuance or simple extinction—that they profess to believe will be their fate through eternity. If an overwhelming majority of Americans believe in the afterlife, it is striking how uncurious they are about the supposedly billions of souls who are presently populating this alternative, presumably better world. Where are they now and what are they doing? You would think they might merit at least an occasional thought or two. That was the point of my two thought experiments—"The First Three Minutes of the Afterlife" and "Afterlife Anonymous"—to stimulate people to think about a wonderfully interesting, if unanswerable question. Too often, human nature being what it is, it is tempting to want to have it both ways (a cop out with which religion, unwittingly or not, frequently colludes): i.e., it offers a consolingly simple, picture-perfect glimpse of the afterlife that cannot be wrong, that requires no thought, only faith.

From this perspective, we can see why the moment of death, the passage from life to death, from existence to non-existence, is seized upon. It is not only unforgettable but the only bridge we can actually experience between one state and the next, between one irrefutable world and a possible, alternative realm. We can also see why the denial of death is such a powerful and satisfying defense mechanism.

Years ago, Abraham Maslow proposed that there is an ascending "hierarchy of needs" governing human behavior, a pyramid in which the most basic biological needs—for reproduction, for self-preservation and survival (and all that goes with it)—are at the bottom and the highest are at the top: the need for self-esteem, for love, for what he would call *self-actualization*. It was his crucial point that the most basic biological needs had to be satisfied *first* before the higher needs could be met. There is of course no more basic need than self preservation. And from that standpoint, it is immediately apparent that the denial of death—providing it does not become *delusional*—is in the service of the biological need for survival. That is, up to the point of actively dying, when something else is required. Furthermore, our unique ability to contemplate our death long before it occurs, provides ample time to symbolize death to our heart's content (one of Maslow's higher needs). We are thus in the paradoxical existential position of having to simultaneously satisfy two deeply contradictory needs: to oppose and deny death in order to insure survival; and to symbolically reflect upon death to satisfy our higher need for understanding.

It is a theme of this book, that for most people, the denial of death prevails.

Thus, Stephanie, who as a teenager could tenderly sit for weeks on end by the bedside of a dying rabbi, twenty years later could not tolerate the sight of her father lying dead in a hospital bed (softly crying while kissing him repeatedly on the cheek): "Please don't be dead, Dad. Don't be dead."

As against this, there is the denial of death that comes across as belligerent defiance. The woman, for example, bitter over having had to tend to her incapacitated mother, her life needlessly prolonged by a feeding tube, unable to overcome her own chronic depression, who says—on the prospect of her own death—"Fear death? I want death!"

And there is the exquisitely sensitive, immensely creative, but very unhappy man who—asked to contemplate his inevitable date with the afterlife—says, "My life has been torture—why should I care?"

In short, the denial of death comes in counterfeit forms and myriad shapes. It is not nearly as surmountable as Elizabeth Kübler-Ross seems to think. Her fifth and final stage of dying—what she calls the acceptance of death—I would call surrender. There comes a point when the processes of death become so overwhelming that it does not seem to make sense to oppose them. The dying animal, or human organism, then surrenders, but that is not the same thing as acceptance of death/the extinction of life and hope/the state of non-existence. It is instead what is called "identification with the aggressor." It is to unconsciously join up with, to submit to a plainly superior force, to call for a brief respite, a truce with an unbeatable opponent. It is to play dead—a universal, favorite ploy among animals as noted long ago by Konrad Lorenz—so as to escape the real thing. It is to control death by imitating it. It is paradoxically to flirt with suicide as a symbolic way of taking charge of life. What it cannot mean is to accept our extinction. How could it?

To see that, imagine a demoralized, dying person who has steadfastly refused a last-resort regimen of chemotherapy; who has gone home from the hospital to die; who, exhausted, has lapsed into a seemingly final stupor. Imagine the very same person, however, against all odds, a few hours later, waking up and feeling inexplicably good; being informed by a bedside doctor that the cancer miraculously has gone into complete remission with no need for further treatment. Could anyone then still opt for the terminal stage of death over this serendipitous, second chance possibility of life?

To wish for anything—even the inevitability of one's death—is to animate it with intentionality. Only someone alive, someone who hopes for something, can do that.

But enough of the afterlife, perhaps you are thinking. What about all those people, those millions of people, who commune with their God on a daily basis? Who talk to Him. Pray to Him. Feel His presence. Perform His rituals. Obey His commands.

It is time to consider the kind of relationship one has when one imagines or believes one is relating to God.

CHAPTER FIVE

THE HIERARCHY OF BELIEFS

Someone who says—"I *know* there is a God"—expresses an affectively charged, non-verbal experience, of which there can be no doubt. In this sense, the believer, sure of everything his senses are telling him, seems to mean, "I know what I experienced."

We all rely on this kind of certitude to make it through the day. This morning, for example, it did not rain, it poured. On the way to the office I was worried that my umbrella, which has seen better days, would not make it through the storm, that I might have to explain to my patients why I got drenched; that the subway line running from Queens where I live to the Manhattan office where I practice might get stalled from flooding, which has happened before, thereby causing me to be late; that my patients, assuming the downpour constitutes a bona fide weather emergency, will not bother to show up; and that the moldering ceiling in the corridor outside my office, leaky to begin with, will finally begin to come down in earnest.

But I don't only worry. I observe, too, I think, I remember, I make many associations to the rain, and I feel varying emotions. I note, for instance, the discarded, wind-broken umbrellas littering the streets, already beginning to disappear under filthy pools of accumulating rain water, and I am finally grateful when I make it to my office before my first patient is scheduled. I'm relieved the corridor ceiling is still in one place, as is my battered umbrella. And once inside my office, feeling safe and secure, a bit like a lucky survivor, I can enjoy the rhythmic beating of the rain against the windowpane, as I usually do.

Making it through the rain to my office in the morning means different things to me, can spark different memories, and engender manifold associations. If I should therefore say to someone—"I know that it rained this morning"—I am doing far more than asserting a simple fact of nature. I am referring to a rich penumbra of experiences that I alone indubitably had, in the particular way that it occurred to me, all of which make the truth of what I claim unassailable.

But could I be wrong? Well, there is always the chance I might be off on the timeline, thinking what had really happened this afternoon had occurred much earlier. I might be exaggerating what was only a very steady rain and a gusty day, into a humongous storm. I might be suffering a more serious memory lapse. It is at least logically possible that what I actually dreamed this morning—when I was in a vivid hypnogogic state—I am confusing with reality. But what are the chances of that? Much less than one in a thousand. Too many experiences, too many interwoven associations speak against it. I am sure I can tell the difference between a whole segment of a waking day and the passage of a fleeting dream, as can almost everyone else. But I also know there are such things as hallucinations, optical illusions, perceptual distortions, thought disorders, which means saying I had a certain experience does not logically constitute proof that what I describe is objectively real.

From that perspective, to say "I believe in God" means "I believe in my experience of God." It is another, profoundly different assertion to say, "My experience of God is a perfectly accurate description of objective reality." Someone who says, "I know there is a God," is therefore not unlike the person who says, "I know my mother loves me." Such a person, often flooded with emotion—under the guise of reporting a fact—is really talking about an overpowering intuition, the feeling of a presence, a connection to an other that can hardly be challenged. Such a person would be wasting his time to seriously doubt that "my mother loves me." But just imagine for a moment a very familiar scenario: a mother who is being treated by a psychiatrist for her chronic depression. In her sessions, she paints the picture of a relationship that her son would be dismayed to hear and find it difficult to comprehend. She talks about how—in spite of her obvious attachment and concern for her sensitive son— she has resented, ever since her husband abandoned her, the burden of being a single parent. She reveals she has found it increasingly hard, sometimes almost impossible, not to be critical of and angry at a son she views as being excessively demanding of her attention and affection. She admits she cannot wait for the day her son moves out of her house, and so on. Examples like this—when our subjectivity speaks to us with seemingly infallible authority—can be multiplied ad infinitum. Think of the woman who "knows that her husband is faithful," but mysteriously does not seem to also know of the numerous affairs he has discreetly and simultaneously carried on for almost as long as they were married. Or, to bring it to the most visceral, concrete level, think of any person, in the presence of whom your flesh begins to crawl and who oddly enough happens to feel the same way about you. Think of how, for example, she sees you as sullen and uncommunicative and you see her as withholding and haughty. How she sees you as pompous and humorless and you see her as hypocritical and vain. Or think of two people locked into an ugly, escalating argument, each subjectively enraged at the other, each willing to swear, each utterly convinced that whatever the other says must be wrong, that what is claimed to be white must be black, what is held to be black must be white.

We either forget or fail to realize that subjective experience is not a simple mirror or photograph of objective reality, whether interpersonal or otherwise. It is a construct and residue, an end product of a long process. It is an indispensable, direct access to what we call our consciousness and our subjectivity (and therein probably our most prized data). But it is not a mirror or photograph of our consciousness either. It is not a reflection of our interpersonal relationships. It is not a copy or record of our preconscious or our unconscious. Our subjective experience, regardless of how compelling it may be, tells us little about the raw data of our impressions, how they emerged from our neurobiology, from our molecular biology, from the quantum mechanical processes which underlie it. Most important of all, we overlook that my subjectivity in all but a handful of cases will radically differ from your subjectivity.

When what we experience is a merging, symbiotic, oceanic feeling, a oneness with whatever is being experienced, we begin to lose the crucial distinction between subjective certainty and objective truth. If we are unwilling to step back from the immediacy of our impressions—differentiate them from what they are supposed to represent and at least consider what another, different experience of the same object or phenomenon might be—we will be unable to establish the kind of consensual validation that is the benchmark of shared truth. We would be fated instead to remain trapped in the solipsism of our own private belief system.

Daniel Dennett is right when he says believers believe in belief. He is wrong when he seems to imply that—because what we are really after is social solidarity (in the Darwinian sense) and group inclusiveness—we want belief for belief's sake. As if simply believing in, say, membership in the Rotary Club, in astrology, or in anything so long as one believes in it, would suffice.

I suggest, instead of belief for the sake of belief, there is something that, following Maslow, might be called a *hierarchy of beliefs*. At the bottom, in the deepest part of our psyche, are the most basic beliefs: the belief in some kind of a primitive relationship to an embracing, cosmic, parental figure, a relationship that exudes oceanic feeling and symbiotic oneness, that alternately imparts a sense that one is being watched over, protected, rescued, loved. Such a belief—in omnipotent parental nurturance—has its roots in a non-verbal and often a pre-verbal experience. Worth mentioning is that such a belief is a deeply satisfying, profoundly positive one. Its flip, negative side is the spooky feeling we get whenever we sense a hostile presence. It is characteristic that we not only move towards and try to merge with the positive belief but feel strongly drawn to it. If we now consider the perspective of the devout believer— who typically will view the committed skeptic as an alien presence, a mean-spirited, cold-hearted rationalist—we can understand their innate opposition. Why would they or anyone, under the sway of such a mesmerizing belief system, ever want to exchange the eternal promise of Jesus' sweet face for the dreariness of such a philosophy? Even if right, what could they possibly gain by embracing such a demoralizing, negative world view?

To make this clearer, here is a hypothetical debate between a believer and a skeptic who are trying to understand one another:

Believer: "You seem to think that science is the royal road to the truth. But there are many sources of truth. There is the truth of poetry. Of dreams. Of literature. Of imagination. And the truth of faith."

Skeptic: "I agree truth can come from myriad by-ways. But I am not talking about the countless triggers of what we agree to call the truth. I'm talking about the best method, the only tried and true method we have for determining the accuracy of any given truth claim, as against the almost infinite possibility for error. True, we can have all the hunches in the world, but if we want to seriously assert that we are describing an important aspect of objective reality, whether inner or outer, at some point we have to bring in the skeptical method. And that means reason as well as intuition, logic as well as imagination, and shared evidence as well as subjective experiences."

Believer: "And I agree that truth has to be differentiated from error. But I emphatically disagree that the presentation and gathering of physical evidence is the only means of establishing the authenticity of the world we live in. I agree the skeptical method is the *sine qua non* for establishing scientific truth. But we have a spiritual as well as a physical existence, there is a spiritual as well as a physical world, and no one to my knowledge has ever arrived at a spiritual truth by means of the skeptical method alone."

Skeptic: "You are, I presume, talking about faith here?"

Believer: "Yes. Faith. Not faith that can move mountains, but faith, in partnership with reason, that is an indispensable guide for reaching the spiritual side of life."

Skeptic: "When you say 'the spiritual side of life,' are you talking about anything more than the indescribable mystical feelings, the noble strivings, that admittedly have characterized our human species from the dawn of recorded time? Are you, for example, talking about supernatural agencies, about miracles, about divine inspiration, about a Biblical God, for example, who supposedly created heaven and earth in a specified number of days?"

Believer: "I am talking about God, but not God in a concrete, literal sense. There may not be many gods, but God reveals himself in many ways. There is a metaphorical God, an abstract, theological God, a God that one prays to, a God that one is comforted by, a God that one questions and a God that one yearns to know."

Skeptic: "Tell me, is there a God who reveals himself not in Biblical miracles, but through physical signs, signs that can be measured and evaluated, reasoned about, tested and are at least theoretically capable of being consensually validated?"

Believer: "And, when necessary, falsified?"

Skeptic: "You are finally understanding me. Yes."

Believer: "If you are asking me, as I think you are, if God can be reduced to a physical quantity, the answer of course is no."

Skeptic: "I am not asking if the essence of God, whatever that is, can be reduced to a physical quantity. I am asking if the means by which we apprehend the physical manifestation of His presence or intervention can be

verified. I am asking the very
questions, except on a much
broader scale, that experienced
investigators of paranormal
phenomena, such as ghosts,
regularly ask. Is there any proof at
all that supernatural agencies
manifest their presence in the
physical world as reported
routinely?"

Believer: "If you are asking if the
soul can be weighed, if the afterlife
can be measured, if heaven can ever
be glimpsed through some kind of
super electron telescope, the answer
is no."

Skeptic: "All I am asking is that
for once in our history, that a single
claim of alleged divine
intervention, of the millions of such
claims that are daily made by
devout believers, be actually
verified by the only means of
verification we know that has stood
the test of time."

Believer: "You obviously do not
accept the massive subjective
testimony of millions of intelligent
believers. You only accept the
weight of mute physical evidence."

Skeptic: "So long as you are
claiming, as I think you are, that

supernatural agencies can make their presence known in physical manifestations, the answer has to be yes. And by physical manifestations, I include, as does every reputable neuroscientist, the entire inner world of our immensely complicated, private subjectivity."

Believer: "I believe in neuroscience, too, but I think people are more than their biology. There is a spiritual or transcendental side, a higher side. The testimony of faith, faith that is fully compatible with reason, is the best evidence we have for this indispensable dimension of the human equation."

Skeptic: "Can you tell me how faith can be compatible with reason, if it is not based upon evidence—evidence that is capable, when faulty, of being falsified?"

Believer: "I know from personal experience and from the testimony of countless others, that faith alone, faith without the necessary help of science, can also reveal the truth."

Skeptic: "And I know from personal experience—not only that I lack such faith—but that there are

> millions of people who have such
> faith, faith of a different persuasion,
> that directly contradicts your
> faith."

We can see that such a debate cannot ever be resolved. They do not agree on what constitutes truth. They do not agree on what evidence is. They do not agree on what should count as belief or what the rules of the game are. Their disagreement runs deeper than an intellectual or metaphysical dispute. Their conflict is psychodynamic, not epistemological.

The skeptic is someone who believes you cannot ask the question—"Is there a God?"—if you are certain you know the answer. You must be prepared to hear an answer you may not like: i.e., "Is there a God?"—"No" or "Maybe" or "Yes, but it is beyond our human capacity to ever have the foggiest idea of what He is like, either in this life or the next." You can, in short, certainly have belief, but you must also have reason and doubt.

The devout believer, by contrast, has a different mindset. He does not value reason less, he values emotion more. He may truly love language and logic, but what most moves him or her tends to be inexpressible. Such difference can best be understood psychodynamically.

The Conversion Experience

In his great classic, *The Varieties of Religious Experience*, William James spoke of: "the feelings, acts and experiences of individual men in their solitude, so far as they apprehend themselves to stand in relation to whatever they may consider the divine." According to his new, radically inclusive definition, one person, alone, could have a religion. James is leading up to his famous concept of the conversion experience, a process he conceives of psychodynamically, although he does not use that term. First there is "the sick soul," the darkness of mind that precedes conversion. Such a person of necessity begins at the bottom. To know the real meaning of life, he or she must taste their own despair. James reveals how, as a young man, he himself was stricken with the blackest despair. Because of experiences like that, what we know, says James, "is that there are dead feelings, dead ideas and cold beliefs, and there are hot and live ones, and when one grows hot and alive within us, everything has to recrystalize about it." (p. 404)

Such is the darkness of mind that precedes conversion. Considered by many to be the founder of the psychology of religion, it is often claimed that what James accomplished was to *psychologize* religion. Conversion, he pointed out, need not be looked at in a narrow sense; the main idea being that an unintegrated self becomes incandescently energized and integrated—made whole. From that perspective, becoming religious is only one way of reaching unity. "The new birth," he says, may be away from religion, towards unbelief. He tells of a man who becomes "converted" to avarice.

Most important for William James is experience. No matter what your religion, each mind and self must filter it through the lens of its own consciousness (we can hear echoes from James' greatest masterpiece, *The Principles of Psychology*). The breadth of James' influence cannot be overestimated. Bill Wilson, the charismatic founder of Alcoholics Anonymous, in a letter to Carl Jung, citing his indebtedness to *The Varieties of Religious Experience*, said that all he did was to make "conversion experiences—nearly every variety reported by James—available on an almost wholesale basis." (p. 405)

In his great intellectual biography—*William James: In the Maelstrom of American Modernism*—Robert Richardson refers to James' "genius for the middle ground." It's a lovely way to say he seems to want to have his cake and eat it, too. Yes, when a genius of his caliber devotes much of his mental life towards balancing the polarities of rigorous experimental psychology and the experiential world of transcendental relatedness, what a glorious thing it can be.

To bring his concept to life, here are two examples of dramatic conversions both to and away from religion.

Towards the end of *The Broken Estate*—his famous critical study of the waning influence of Christianity upon Western literature—James Wood talks about his own crisis of faith. Indoctrinated as a child by his zealous parents into the evangelical branch of the Church of England, he grew up witnessing the "manifestation of the Spirit." He saw people speaking in tongues, ecstatically worshipping, prophesying, being the recipient of alleged healing miracles. He watched first hand people dancing in the aisles, whirling and writhing. It was explained to him afterwards that these dancers were "taken with the Spirit."

But at fifteen, there were doubts that could not be so easily answered. No sick person, he noticed, was really "ever healed of anything." He had been a born-again Christian, but while only a teenager, he became an atheist. It was, he would say, looking back, "easy to do." He had sat down with a notebook of paper and written the four or five objections he could think of to believing in God. The liberation he would feel from his subsequent loss of faith was a youthful blessing from which he would not look back.

What James Wood is describing is what William James presciently called a conversion towards unbelief. Although an early convert to skepticism, James Wood would not lose his fascination with the spiritual side of even the most fanatical of religions. In spite of its excesses, he can respect evangelicalism for the "intensity" with which it imbues the act of choosing and the consequences that stem from it. Philosophy cannot kill God, he notes, but only a rival belief—the belief that God does not exist. In this regard, James Wood seems no less passionate about his atheism than is Richard Dawkins. Not surprisingly, Dostoyevsky is a favorite author, ultimately a believer, a practicing Christian who, paradoxically, can present some of the most profound objections to his own beliefs. Citing *The Brothers Karamazov*, James Wood says that his parable of The Grand Inquisitor "is, for me, an unanswerable attack on the cruelty of God's hiddenness." (p. 254)

He goes on to consider some of the classic objections to the skeptical position: What wisdom can it offer, other than a counsel to despair? What consolation can it give that can compare to the Christian promise of eternal salvation? What is there to look forward to, what is there to celebrate, if one views death as the terminator of all life and hope?

Refusing to flinch from the tragic limitations which skepticism unavoidably imposes on life, James Wood defiantly answers (p. 254), the advantage "is that the false purpose has at least been invented by man, and one can strip it away to reveal the actual pointlessness." He adds that he for one does not believe that the strength of Christianity lies in the comfort and consolations it offers. The only strength it can possibly offer is that "it is true."

He agrees that the best defense against the Problem of Evil has been the necessity for free will; but then caustically asks, how would you know a world without free will, is a poorer world, than one with free will (plus evil and suffering)? He admits on the one hand that a world without free will, one in which God controlled all our actions, would be morally less interesting than our present world. But he reminds us of the famous argument against free will raised by the seventeenth century skeptic, Peter Bayle: why would God grant a gift that He knows in advance will ultimately serve to bring about the destruction of the person to whom it is given? What kind of mother would permit her daughter to attend a ball, for example, knowing in advance her daughter was going to be seduced and raped?

Might it not be better, perhaps, asks James Wood, to have a world with a little less free will, but also less pain and less evil? Would not the world be then more like heaven? What is the necessity for using the earth as a testing ground for admission to heaven? Why must we live before heaven?

James Wood ends his meditation with what, for me, is the most compelling, searing sentence in the entire book (p. 263): "Why must we move through this unhappy, painful, rehearsal for heaven, this desperate antechamber, this foreword written by an anonymous author, this hard prelude in which so few of us can find our way?"

Let me add a few questions of my own to James Wood's searching inquiry. Why not a world with free will, but one in which *everyone freely chooses good* because God—knowing in advance what their choices will be—only allows the fetuses or embryonic souls of good people to survive? Or a world of saints—in which there could be endless temptation and wrestling with one's soul—but ultimately only saints? Or a world that is literally like a City of Angels?

Finally, if it is necessary to have free will in order to have moral agency, then why would it not also be necessary to have free will in the transcendental state of highest spirituality in heaven?

Which immediately revises the paradoxical question—does God have free will? If He does not, He cannot be omnipotent. If He does, then He has at least the capability, if He chooses, of doing evil; and a God, who was capable of evil, even though He would never actually do it, cannot be an infinitely good God.

The paradox becomes clearer if we consider the ordinary person or soul, as it is believed to exist in heaven or hell. If they have no free will, then their actions are even more controlled by God than they would be on earth. For, in the afterlife, where there is direct contact with God, there is no need for faith. Imagine now a being, with free will, someone in heaven but with the freedom to choose good or evil. Could he or she ever choose evil in such a circumstance? The answer would have to be yes; if they could not, they would not have free will. But what would an evil choice conceivably be in heaven? Well, of course, it would be one of sheer perversity, one that would make little sense, other than to satisfy a wicked craving to defy God, undermine His authority, and sabotage the happiness of the perhaps too complacent surrounding souls, to shake them up—such would be the nature of evil. But now consider the person or soul in hell, who has been granted free will. Who in that position, with the clear evidence of their everlasting folly constantly before their eyes, would not *freely* choose to reverse their fate, be good, and, if possible, go to heaven or at least get out of hell?

We see why such questions are unanswerable and why—in all but the rarest of cases—they are avoided at all costs by almost everyone.

One such exception, my second example of a dramatic conversion both to and away from religion, is the great American scientist, Edward O. Wilson.

In his touching narrative memoir, *Naturalist*, he describes his upbringing. Like James Wood, he had been introduced at an

early age to evangelical Protestantism, Pensacola's First Baptist
Church. He is impressed that they do not waste time with
philosophy, that instruction and ritual are minimal, that belief
is all, that Jesus is always with you, and that He will return.

Decades later, looking back on his youthful conversion—but
now a world famous scientist trying to understand and explain
religion as a natural phenomenon—he will say, admiringly (p.
38), "It catches the power."

Edward O. Wilson is not only evocative but nostalgic as he
describes the passionately idealistic teenage boy who waits in
line to be baptized, to be born again; who, awe-struck, patently
submits to the meant-to-be-life-changing baptism process (to
be literally dunked by the pastor in a chest-high tank of water);
but who immediately thereafter drifts away and can only
ruefully note (p. 43) "Something somewhere cracked."

Unlike James Wood, Edward O. Wilson is not tortured about
religion. About the most assertive thing he has to say is (p. 45),
"I could never accept that science and religion are separate
domains." But he also reveals, years later how—invited to
attend a moving evangelical service in honor of the Rev. Martin
Luther King, he surprised himself by silently weeping (p. 46):
"My people, I thought. My people. What else lay hidden deep
within my soul?"

If we take them at their testimony, James Wood and Edward
O. Wilson had positive conversion experiences both towards
and away from belief. The overwhelming majority of reported
conversion experiences are of this nature, positive experiences
that move towards something that unifies. Even when the
conversion is towards disbelief, it is invariably described as one
of liberation and release.

From the standpoint of the hierarchy of beliefs, we can see the
conversion experience represents the full package, touching on

just about every primary need. The need to be saved, to be protected, to be watched over, to be nurtured, to be loved. The need to meditate on our impending death, allay our fears, and symbolize the longed-for afterlife in a way that can be grasped. If we liken the conversion experience to music—inasmuch as it often reaches inexpressible depths—we can think of it as chords, not notes, evoking several or many things at once in us in a harmonious, seemingly magical unity.

But, of course, this is a psychological, not a metaphysical or even a philosophical study. We are searching for a more secular explanation, one rooted in human nature, for the almost universal longing for communion with a transcendental other. Fortunately, we do not have far to look.

The Oceanic Feeling

Freud never had it, but most people do. The starry skies above, the majesty of a sunset, the immensity of the ocean. Although the feeling is often used as a gateway to a mystical, transcendental vision of nature, it does not have to be. It is a simple sense of being overcome and momentarily lost in the splendor and beauty of what you are looking at, of seeming insignificant in comparison with what surrounds you, of wanting to be part of it, to merge with it, of suspended time and serendipitous serenity. People of faith imbue the oceanic feeling with self-evident religious meaning, but secular, nature-loving scientists are no less susceptible to it. It is characteristic of the oceanic feeling that it is transient, it comes on its own terms, and it tends to be something that most people would rather experience than talk about.

In his classic psychoanalytic study of early mother-child relations, *The Shadow of the Object*, Christopher Bollas first introduced his famous concept of *the transformational object*: (p. 14) "A transformational object is experientially identified by the infant with processes that alter self experience." This first transformational object, of course, is the mother. The infant who cannot yet identify the mother as a separate person, will nevertheless experience her as a process equated with internal and external transformations. The rapid changes the newborn infant must undergo—emotional, biological, cognitive, environmental—will be initially identified more as a process than a person. The early mother will be known in a symbiotic way, not as a particular person but as a "recurrent experience of being." Bollas means this mother will be primarily experienced as a "process of transformation."

According to Bollas, this fundamental early form of relating will cast its long shadow well into adult life. The person, under the spell of the transformational object, will unconsciously seek out experiences that seem to promise a magical transformation of the self, one that will echo this primary, earliest experience. Such a transformative experience can be a new job, a perfect woman. Typically the person pursues the experience in order to surrender to it. Although the person looks towards the future, as Bollas points out, what is being sought is actually a pre-verbal, pre-symbolic existential memory of a symbiotic transformation of the self.

We immediately see that this search—in the future—for the unconscious memory of the first transformational object (with the mother) could well be the basis for what will later be called the conversion experience. And indeed in another magnificent chapter, *The Spirit of the Object as the Hand of Fate*, Bollas spells this out. The transformational object when found is nominated as sacred. The person feels captured by the object. Time stops. Both the object and the experience surrounding it are imbued with a strange aesthetic. It can be a perfect poem, place, relationship, a magical gambling adventure (i.e., Dostoyevsky's *The Gambler*).

From the standpoint of our theme, it is important that he is offering an insight and possible explanation—one rooted in human nature—for an experience often thought to be transcendental. As compelling and ingenious as I find the idea of the transformational object to be, it may be wrong. Or as our unflappable hypothetical Believer might argue:

> "There may be a transformational object,
> but that in no way precludes the
> possibility that God put it there."

What we cannot be in doubt about, is that millions and millions of Americans claim to be in regular, even daily communion with the presence or spirit of God. The question arises—if the conversion experience does not have an objective transcendental basis—how is this possible?

Relating To God

Let me reiterate I am not a theologian or metaphysical philosopher. In what follows I merely take seriously the claim of those who believe they have contact or are in regular communion with the presence or spirit of God. I leave open the question of what the nature of such a hypothetical supernatural being might be, but I carefully consider what it would entail, what it would mean for *a human being to make a human response* to such a hypothetical being. Although I have read widely and to a certain extent written about areas related to this central theme, what I say is primarily based on the thousands of patients I have seen over the past thirty years. It is possible that those who have told me that they experienced a genuine transcendental connection, have mysteriously undergone a kind of inner transformation that simply cannot be observed. If so, I obviously could not and have not seen it. What I have seen is patients who—while talking with the deepest feelings about God—*seem utterly and only human.* Which does not preclude the possibility that a supernatural being is reaching out and touching them. It just means, that howsoever they are being touched, they are responding in a *human* way.

So the question for me becomes, if a human being is really going to try to have a long-lasting, meaningful and intimate relationship with an omniscient, omnipotent, and infinitely good God, what would be required? In *Knowing If It Is The Real Thing* (Alper, 2003) and in *Self-Defense in a Narcissistic World* (Alper, 2004), I explore in depth the essential elements of intimacy for the ordinary person and the ramification of being caught in an unsymmetrical relationship. Here I summarize some key points and see how they apply to our theme.

So, what does it really mean, from a human perspective, to attempt to have a relationship with a supernatural being? First, what cannot be ignored is that a relationship with a deity is a relationship with a being you never see or experience in any of the ways you interact with everyone else. It is a relationship in which—although every aspect of your self or soul is known in advance—you cannot know (and are considered presumptuous to even try to guess) a single thought or feeling of the Other. Not only is there almost nothing in common, there is an infinite developmental divide separating the believer and his or her God. Is it even possible, therefore, to empathize and with whom?

While it is, of course, taken for granted there are profound differences between religious and interpersonal intimacy, it is illuminating to articulate them. For example, the entire life of a religious person can be viewed, from a certain metaphysical perspective, as a spiritual performance or test, upon which final judgment will be passed in the afterlife. But other than the gift of life, nothing more is to be required from God. Although prayers can be offered, no demands can be made. A believer, traditionally, is to be faithful to only one God who, however, is free to have a similar relationship with billions of others. There can be no direct expression and interchange of emotion within the context of the ongoing religious relationship and, of course, no simple, sensuous (tactile) comforting. Such a relationship, it is more accurate to say, is one of searching, rather than having. Not surprisingly, love for a being as hidden as God is expressed—not in spontaneous interacting—but through meditative acts of worship.

But what of the part that is assigned in the religious relationship to God? While the issues about to be raised, for all I know may have already been thoroughly debated in arcane tracts by theologians, they are by no means in the forefront of the consciousness of the typical believer. This may be because they have not been taught, are not thought relevant to the practice of faith, and, perhaps most important of all, are not readily understandable. Yet, to some extent, in my view they are considered in the unconscious of every believer.

Here, then, from a psychological point of view, are the critical questions that are rarely raised, at least publicly, in traditional religious circles. Does any benefit or growth accrue to God from His seemingly passionate involvement with human beings? Does He ever express needs, or only demands? Can it be that God may want, but does not need the love of people? Is there room in such an odd couple—person and Deity—for spontaneity, playfulness, engagement—or is the relationship as such, and in the afterlife to come, to be only one of witness and presence? Does the essence of a Divinity allow for a sense of humor?

Why does the Bible portray two different Gods, with two different personalities? The Jehovah of the Old Testament expresses anger, rage, jealousy, a desire for vengeance. He renders judgment, expresses fierce disapproval and savagely punishes enemies. By contrast, the God of the New Testament emphasizes love and forgiveness. Especially interesting, however, are the emotions and states of mind that the Bible does not show God as having: indecision, doubt, vulnerability, anxiety, fear and happiness. For, as a psychodynamic and psychoanalytic psychotherapist, it is at least worth asking—does God have an unconscious? And if not, as I think is suggested in the Bible, can He still experience shock, surprise or relief?

By contrast, the God of religious dogma in His relationship to humankind is primarily revealed through displays of divine approval or disapproval. He is depicted as self-contained, grateful to no one or nothing; masculine in gender, as Father or incarnated Son, but without a specific sexual identity, character or personality. He is not only never ill and never tempted— except for His brief sojourn as Christ on earth—but is presumably immune from disease. Other than His original struggle with Satan, He does not experience conflict. One can only wonder what kind of relationship is possible with a Deity that is squarely beyond the pale of human experience? Such a question is compounded by the fact there is no other God with whom to compare this historical God (other than the gods of comparative religion) and therefore no room for discrimination and choice. Add to this, the fact that traditionally the question of faith is not presented as an option. From the very beginning, the initiate is taught that there is no such thing as honest skepticism. There is only belief, a state of grace, or the mortal sin of the atheist's despair. The initiate cannot disbelieve, must love and cannot abandon the practice of the religion that has been passed on without incurring a formidable punishment.

It is immediately apparent for all of these reasons—from a purely psychodynamic point of view—the relationship between a believer and his or her God is subject to remarkable constraints. Foremost may be the extraordinary mystery that surrounds it, in which much of the time is necessarily spent trying to pin it down, to fathom and gather one's true thoughts and feelings towards God, while attempting to guess how God views the person or may at the dreaded time of reckoning. It could be said therefore, as a relationship—one that cannot be fully realized before the afterlife—it never really begins, but is rather a preparation, an expectation or fantasy of what such a beginning might be (as clearly implied in the famous question—"What would you say were you to meet God?"). It follows that a good part of a religious person's fear of God comes from his or her uncertainty as to what ultimately lies behind the mystery of existence. Or to put it another way, the believer can't help at times but be haunted by the question—just how friendly, understanding, empathic will the God one eventually meets really be?

For all the above reasons, the relationship depicted in religious dogma—especially in light of the concept of original sin—can at times be seen as one of profound mutual distrust. If, on the one hand, from the perspective of God (as imagined, of course, by an infinitely fallible human being)—at any moment a given person, by exercising free will and choosing evil, is capable of falling into original sin—it is hard to see how much confidence He can have in humankind. If, on the other hand, from the point of view of mere mortals—where ordinary acts of evil are theoretically punishable by sentencing to some kind of hell—where is there room to relax and how can there be such a thing as an acceptable mistake? Can, for example, God be offended and not resort to punitive action? Or, considering the stakes are so high, are mistakes and the concept of working on a relationship irrelevant, and only sins, their confession and possible forgiveness the only thing that matters? If so, it is hard to see, from the standpoint of the believer, how one can trust a Deity who never gives feedback, about whom you are perpetually clueless about what He really thinks and feels about you, and who applies an infinitely high standard of morality to your behavior that may or may not be tempered by equal measures of infinite love and mercy.

Just how do you love a Being who wields such incredible power over you and whom you fear so much? Looked at this way, the relationship seems fundamentally based on morality, on issues of good and evil, rather than, as is the case between ordinary people, on the interest and pleasure that is generated by the encounter. It follows, if what is up for grabs is whether one's soul is to be saved or not, then nothing else seems important.

Yet, although it seems self-evident that the believer would perennially be troubled by questions of his or her faith in the existence and ultimate goodness of God, no one apparently is threatened by the quality of God's faith in people. There is no expectation of God trusting that a particular person who, say, has just committed a mortal sin will sooner or later come to his or her senses. Instead, God, with divine patience, waits to see whether the exercise in free will results in good or evil acts (although paradoxically He knows this already) and then, supposedly responds with corresponding approval (love and forgiveness) or disapproval (readiness to punish).

It is clear that what is missing from this conventional portrait of a divine persona, is the recognition of the profound and pervasive ambivalence that characterizes all human relations, especially transcendental ones. Although purity of heart is traditionally demanded from would-be believers, that is exactly what no human really has. Where is the empathy for the ordinary person, neither good nor evil, who struggles but does not reach any unambiguous stance vis-à-vis religious belief and commitment? The fact that mankind's relationship to God is primarily cast in the trappings of a cosmic morality play—with archetypal principles of good and evil battling for the soul of the person, with God waiting and watching, the all-seeing Judge, occasionally intervening with revelations, miracles, stupendous acts of grace, forgiveness—hides the basic psychological truth that so far as interpersonal relations are concerned, there does not seem room for commonplace, undramatic failure, indecision, confusion, lack of development, stubborn refusal to change, demoralization, withdrawal. In other words, there does not seem to be recognition of all the impediments to the achievement of genuine intimacy that universally frustrate people, and especially there does not seem to be nearly enough room to work on all the daunting, extraordinary obstacles to religious intimacy in a human, non-miraculous fashion.

For example, is there room in the transcendental domain for dissent, for the one who cannot or will not believe? If perhaps the greatest possible repudiation of what was supposed to be a romantic, intimate commitment is the retrospective disclaimer, "I never loved you"—analogously the gravest rebuke of an erstwhile religious devotee is the declaration, "I do not believe in the existence of God." This is far weightier than the former, human, all-too-human case, not only because the object of worship is supposedly of infinitely greater significance, but because the denial is totalistic, encompassing even prior existence: at least the rejecting person who proclaims, "I never loved you" does not deny that both participants once truly existed. (This is one powerful reason why the disbeliever's fear of divine retribution can be so unsettling—if a mistake has been made, and one can never prove God does not exist, then one has unwittingly delivered the ultimate metaphysical insult to God.)

But the question immediately suggests itself—how can someone love God, while simultaneously dreading Him? Is it possible somehow to love God without fearing Him at all? Can it be ever appropriate to be angry with or to express anger at God? Is it possible to have a close relationship to Him and yet be independent of His approval? Can someone, who has been deeply religious, suddenly initiate a divorce—perhaps a trial separation—from God without incurring divine retribution? Can a person, other than praying for help, request (say for the purpose of clarification) some autobiographical information concerning God? Is it possible to have a non-reverent or a playfully irreverent, relaxed time with one's Deity? Or can one acknowledge God's omnipotence and yet, howsoever irrationally, quarrel with particular instances of its manifestation? How then, finally, does one challenge an infinite being? (And yet, of course, one does by defiantly insisting on one's right to think small—that is, to be narcissistic.)

I realize, as I have mentioned, that this strange catalogue of questions I have been raising—especially those speculating upon God's point of view regarding human beings—are almost never broached, if at all, outside of esoteric theological tracts.

This is not, I believe, because they are considered heretical, but because they are manifestly unanswerable and do not seem to go anywhere. My point is the fact they are inscrutable does not prevent them—howsoever dimly and unconsciously—from being considered. And the more deeply religious a person is, the more difficult it is to avoid the shadow of such questions. If we think about it from the perspective of the true believer— the fate of whose soul possibly throughout all of eternity is at stake, but where there is absolutely no divine feedback—who can traditionally only know the verdict when it is too late to do anything about it, on Judgment Day, it is impossible not to be susceptible, to a greater or lesser extent, to a desperate need to at least guess how one's God may feel or think about him or her.

For all of the above reasons, it is hardly surprising that the overwhelming number of patients postpone thinking about such matters for as long as possible. When they do, they tend to quickly get discouraged. From a pragmatic standpoint, it can all seem so pointless. They can neither prove nor disprove the existence of the afterlife and of a supreme being. At the earliest they must wait until they die for a final answer, and no one has ever come back from the dead to report on their findings. The sensible, practical thing to do seems to make the very most of one's life while here and do what one reasonably can to delay the inevitability of one's death.

Such would seem to be the unspoken logic of our most basic, biological need for survival. From an evolutionary perspective, it is hard to see what can be adaptive or useful in dwelling on our extinction. Which may be why in over thirty years I have not encountered a single patient who had a conversion experience in the life-altering sense of William James. I do not doubt such experiences occur, but they are rarely seen by mental health professionals, and when they are, they tend to be chronicled by neurologists and specialists such as Oliver Sacks (who in turn are likely to offer at least plausible accounts of how sudden physical changes in the brain—oxygen deprivation, etc.—can result in the most utterly bizarre, out-of-body hallucinations, near death experiences or astounding personality changes).

By contrast, what will impress a psychotherapist such as myself, is just how normal patients seem when they talk about death, the afterlife or God. They may be intensely emotional, their state of mind uncharacteristically existential, but they do not seem in any way different from other patients. They may profess contact with a non-physical, spiritual side of life, but when they do so, they invariably *seem only human and nothing more*.

Of course, there may always be an indiscernible, transcendental aspect to what is being said, to which I am simply not privy.

That raises a final question:

Since we can neither prove nor disprove, nor reach any shared, consensual validation of the existence of non-physical, supernatural forces or agencies; since there can be nothing biologically adaptive, useful or pragmatic in investing our energies in such a project—what is the point of attempting to do so?

To which my own answer would be: There is more to life than the pursuit of equanimity, adaptability and a kind of tensionless nirvana on earth. There is the recognition of (one of Maslow's highest needs) the tragic dimension of life. There is the need to appreciate the poignantly transient nature of everything we most value. There is the sense that it is the guiding meaning which we either construct or find that makes our lives worth living. And there is the primal, physical yearning—regardless of whatever may actually be out there—for a spiritual connection to a cosmic Other.

CHAPTER SIX

GOD AND THE BRAIN

In a chapter called "God and the Limbic System" (in *Phantoms In The Brain*), the brilliant neuroscientist, V.S. Ramachandran, presents what he thinks may be the "first brain experiment ever done on religion directly" (p. 186). His own interest was sparked when he heard what happened when Dr. Michael Persinger, the Canadian psychologist—while experimenting with a transcendental magnetic stimulator—chose to stimulate part of his own temporal lobes. To Dr. Persinger's amazement, he, as he would put it, experienced God for the first time in his life.

Perhaps even more impressive to V.S. Ramachandran, was that Dr. Persinger had never been known to suffer from temporal lobe seizures. He was, oddly enough, just a normal guy. He was unlike those patients with epileptic seizures which originate in the left temporal lobe and can lead to intense spiritual experiences, experiences which can spill over into the non-seizure part of the brain. Such a person, V.S. Ramachandran tells us, was Dostoyevsky.

Ingeniously, he lays out the critical thinking leading up to his daring experiment. He knows that the limbic system is geared mainly toward the experience and expressions of emotions and that knowledge about the function of the limbic system has come from patients who have suffered from epileptic seizures originating in this part of the brain. "Focal, epileptic seizures, however (as opposed to grand mal) can remain confined largely to a single small patch of brain." He notes that in the limbic system, it can happen that "feelings are on fire" (p. 179). (Women have been known to experience orgasm) and on occasion there can even be the "feeling of divine presence and the sense that they are in direct communion with God" (p. 179). Although such feelings typically last for a few seconds each time, they can permanently alter a patient's personality. Nevertheless, they remain a minority phenomenon, "an all or nothing phenomenon."

A concept that may be key in understanding this is kindling: the process whereby a sufficiently intense stimulation of certain neural tracts—such as can occur in an epileptic seizure—can place them in a state of elevated readiness and receptivity ("salience"). These changes can give rise to what some neurologists have called the "temporal lobe personality." Such patients have heightened emotions and can read the most grandiose significance in the most trivial of events. They tend to be "humorless, full of self-importance, and to maintain elaborate diaries that record quotidian events in elaborate detail—a trait called hypergraphia" (p. 180).

Such a patient, V.S. Ramachandran notes, was Paul, a thirty-two-year-old assistant manager of a local Goodwill store who claimed to have had his first seizure when he was eight years old. A few years later he had several additional seizures that transformed his entire life. V.S. Ramachandran wondered if an explanation lay in kindling: what might happen if spurious signals stemming from limbic seizure activity were to spill over and travel to sensory centers (vision and hearing). Then *"every object and event—not just salient ones—would become imbued with deep significance so that the patient would see 'the universe in a grain of sand' and hold 'infinity in the palm of his hand'" (p. 183).

V.S. Ramachandran decided to test directly the hypothesis of kindling—"the notion that kindling has indiscriminately strengthened all connections from the temporal cortex to the amygdala." If correct, all objects presented to a subject, whether trivial or significant, would elicit an approximately equal emotional response in the limbic system as measured by the GSR (galvanic skin response).

To test this hypothesis, V.S. Ramachandran invited two colleagues, specializing in the diagnosis and treatment of epilepsy, to recruit two patients suffering from manifest "temporal lobe epilepsy." The volunteer patients were then seated in front of a computer, with electrodes attached to their hands. Random samples of various types of words and images— ordinary inanimate objects, both familiar and unfamiliar faces, sexually stimulating pictures, four-letter words, scenes of graphic violence, religious, iconic words such as "God"—were shown. If the kindling hypothesis were correct, there would be a more or less strong response to each of the categories. But to their "amazement," V.S. Ramachandran and his colleagues discovered an elevated response primarily to religious words and icons. Not only was there no general enhancement of all categories but, surprisingly, there was "a selective amplification of response to religious words" (p. 186).

As a result of this experiment, it was now clear to V.S. Ramachandran that there are circuits in the human brain that are involved in religious experience and, at least in some epileptics, become demonstrably hyperactive. He concludes philosophically that we are a long way from showing "that there is a 'God module' in the brain that might be genetically specified, but to me the exciting idea is that one can even begin to address questions about God and spirituality scientifically" (p. 188).

From the standpoint of our theme, we can see that V.S. Ramachandran is painstaking in his efforts to be fair to religion. Could God be speaking to us directly through the God module, he wonders? Is there even such a thing as a God module? He hesitates to hazard a guess here and he is equally reluctant to label as unhealthy, those baffling autistic savants, who display extraordinary, if limited, specialized talents. In this regard, he is like Oliver Sacks, who time and again has given us astonishingly empathic tales of patients who have been neurologically traumatized; patients he uncannily refuses to see as psychically damaged and deficient (see his latest remarkable offering, "A Neurologist's Notebook: A Bolt From The Blue," the unforgettable story of a successful orthopedic surgeon, hit by lightning, who thereafter inexplicably develops an unprecedented, all-consuming, lifelong mystical passion for music (July 23, 2007 issue of *The New Yorker*).

Few temporal lobe epileptics have been as noteworthy as Fyodor Dostoyevsky and none has ever written as memorably on the conversion experience. The preeminent Dostoyevsky scholar, Joseph Frank, is right when he says that the character of Prince Myshkin in *The Idiot* is the single greatest study of the inner torment of the epileptic in all of Western literature.

My only point is to reiterate that therapists do not encounter conversion experiences like this. Even world famous experts like V.S. Ramachandran and Oliver Sacks, who specialize in the outer limits of human behavior, rarely see such patients. So what do therapists see? They see patients, the great majority of whom not only believe there is something more to the world than the physical—but who very much want there to be; who are palpably confused when it comes to articulating what this "something more" is; who have only a dream-like conception of what the afterlife might be; who are ambivalent at best when it comes to what heaven and hell might be even if the religion they believe in tells them explicitly what it is; who conceive of God, when they think of Him, essentially as a kind of evanescent presence, an oceanic peacefulness that comforts and envelopes them; who almost never look forward to the afterlife, but invariably fear it; and who rarely reflect on their own behavior—except when they feel they are deserving of genuine punishment or rebuke—in terms of what God may or may not think of them.

What therefore most strikes me about patients who claim to be in communion with a personal God is not the hypocrisy but the *ordinariness* of their behavior. I can detect no significant difference between patients who are religious and those who are not. They are not discernibly more moral, law abiding, honest, conscientious, trustworthy, empathic or kind. They do not necessarily make better husbands, wives, fathers, mothers, sons and daughters. They do not make more noteworthy contributions to the community at large. They do not exhibit healthier self-esteem, stand up to adversity with greater resolve, nor do they manifest more faith in either themselves or other people.

The question arises, then, why not? Why isn't someone presumably in direct contact on a fairly regular basis with a supremely greater source of spiritual strength, manifestly more empowered than his or her less spiritually nourished neighbor? You would think that behavior that is supernaturally guided or inspired would in some way be demonstrable in the real world, clearly distinguishable from the more secular kind, but such is not the case. In fact, in many ways, what we see is the reverse. The closer people come to a mystical Oneness with God, the more seriously out of touch with reality they seem. The more radically they approach the evangelical goal of "living in the Spirit," the less psychologically balanced they seem. The more they attain a state of permanent religious ecstasy, the more they resemble a "temporal lobe personality." (Of course, this is not to deny there are genuine, saint-like people, but only that they are extraordinarily rare.)

The irony, however, seems lost on V.S. Ramachandran that patients such as Paul who—unlike the rest of us—could see "the universe in a grain of sand and hold infinity in the palm of his hand," simultaneously (as he himself notes) "tend to be humorless, full of self-importance and to maintain elaborate diaries that record quotidian events in elaborate detail—a trait called hypergraphia."

Can there be a greater contradiction than seeing the universe in a grain of sand and being humorless and full of self-importance? Lost sight of is that there are no shortcuts to genuine spiritual profundity. There is a world of difference between the conversion experience of a William James—one of the greatest and most enduring of American geniuses—and a temporal lobe personality such as Paul. Even more illuminating is the dramatic example of Fyodor Dostoyevsky: an epileptic who as a young political prisoner in Siberia was first sentenced to be executed before a firing squad, then diabolically granted an eleventh hour reprieve, and who would subsequently develop a lifelong spiritual quest. Yet compare how Dostoyevsky went on to explore the fathomless depths of religious symbolism with the pointlessly grandiose pronouncements of the typical temporal lobe personality. Look at the incredible spiritual complexity of the epileptic Prince Myshkin in comparison with the platitudinous transcendentalism of a Paul. It misses the point to say Dostoyevsky was a genius and the others were not.

The point is that while both may have begun with a traumatic injury to their brain, and perhaps permanent shock to their nervous system, only one person went beyond the neurological event (Maslow's most basic, biological need) to developmentally transform what had happened.

If we consider Bollas' model of the transformational object, or V.S. Ramachandran's model of a possible God module—as a tool for understanding the conversion experience—we should remember that both are rooted in a primitive biological and psychological substratum: Bollas in the earliest mother-infant dyad and V.S. Ramachandran in hypothetically specialized religious tracts of the brain. Both models, in other words, begin somewhere at the bottom of Maslow's hierarchy of needs. That may be why the majority of people who claim to have conversion experiences strike one as being so often out of whack—when measured against the lofty sentiments they swear by.

One thing a therapist soon learns is that there is little romance in being emotionally, psychologically, biologically or neurologically impaired. But I can hear now the insistent voice of the ever vigilant believer, quick to defend the rights of the transcendentalist:

> "If you are looking for evidence of communication with God, you are looking for meaning, not examples of interpersonal behavior. If you honestly want to find manifestations of the spirit, you have to start with the spiritual side of life. You can't do that unless you are first open to the possibility of a spiritual presence. If you begin with the

assumption that you can only believe in
that which has been proven, you can, of
course, nullify spirituality but you are
doing so by fiat, not reason."

Someone who considers herself very much open to the
possibility of supernatural presences is Mary Roach, an
adventurous investigative reporter who is not afraid to go where
others fear to tread. In *Spook: Science Tackles the Afterlife*, she
explores some of the biggest questions of all. She starts out, she
tells us, as a skeptic who wishes there was an afterlife, but who
needs evidence either for or against it. In the past she believes
that skeptics have tended to approach questions regarding
paranormal phenomena as though they already knew the answer.
She is determined to be more open-minded (perhaps
overlooking that she herself seems to begin with the assumption
that skeptics traditionally have been biased against the afterlife).

At the end of the book, Mary Roach asks herself forthrightly,
"So, what do I believe after a year?" She has rigorously
investigated the claims of a rich medley of paranormal
researchers—from cranks who are obsessed with precisely
weighing the soul to data-driven, reputable physical scientists
employing the most high tech equipment available to detect
the faintest electromagnetic emanations coming from the other
side. Her conclusion, she says, is that she has wound up
believing not that "something more" exists but that there is
"something more that science doesn't know." She is especially
impressed with reports of "near death" experiences: the dying
mafia gangster, for example, who, experiencing for the very first
time the presence of God and His unconditional love,
miraculously recovers and subsequently leaves his crime family.
She repeats the oft-noted observation that such experiences are

life-changing and echoes William James when she points to their undeniable pragmatic effects.

Yet, I would like to comment, that is hardly surprising. If the profound need underlying the universal yearning for an afterlife is the need in times of dire extremity for cosmic rescue and love, then—the uncanny experience of such a need being serendipitously answered—cannot help but reinforce the belief in such a Cosmic Being. From that perspective, "near death" experiences can quality as legitimate conversion experiences.

And from a philosophical standpoint, it could be objected that Mary Roach is choosing to conclude her study with yet another variant of the fallacious "God of the gaps" argument (the claim that any time you run up against something that baffles you, you have grounds for smuggling in a supernatural explanation of one sort or another). In contrast to what Mary Roach is saying, however, science is based on the belief that there is always "something more that they (science) doesn't know." If that were not the case, there would be no point to further investigation. It is a cardinal axiom of science that every answer brings in its wake a host of new and deeper questions.

Admittedly, it can sound profound, mysterious and provocative to say "there is something more that science doesn't know." The implication is that there are truths waiting to be discovered that we cannot presently conceive of or imagine, and that such truths, if discovered, may one day overturn even the most cherished assumption of contemporary scientists. *But science already knows this, indeed such has been the history of scientific discoveries.*

The question therefore is not whether there is something more to be known, but when "something more" is discovered, as it is every day in science, will it prove so radical as to constitute a revolution; i.e., the long sought-after proof that consciousness survives in the afterlife? Or will it instead be something that—as have most great discoveries in the past—demolish one or two overdue and outdated theories while leaving intact the essential foundation of science, which, ultimately, always seems to advance?

Finally, if Mary Roach's implication is, as it seems to be, that one day the "something more that science doesn't know" may shake up the foundation of science—where is the proof of that, other than pointing to some intriguing (God of the gaps) oddities? We would do well to remind ourselves of that wise old scientific adage, "extraordinary claims require extraordinary evidence" (which, by the way, is just what no paranormal investigator has ever been able to supply).

The Will To Understand

William James famously said that his "first act of free will should be to believe in free will." In his posthumously published Gifford lectures—*The Varieties of Scientific Experience: A Personal View of the Search for God*—Carl Sagan wishes to replace James' will to believe with his own will to understand. As opposed to other skeptics, he does not see the need for either antagonism or a compartmentalization of science and religion. To him, science is just "informed worship." Worthy of awe and inspiration are the great truths to be discovered, not the grandeur of some imagined Omnipotent Creator. True spirituality is to be equated with the appreciation and proper humility before the immense richness of the universe; a universe much vaster and more complex than the theological one of Aristotle.

As his widow and longtime collaborator, Ann Druyan, notes in her moving introduction, "Carl didn't want just to believe.

He wanted to know. And this would apply, even when it came to facing his own cruel fate:" finally succumbing to pneumonia after enduring three bone marrow transplants.

Reading his book, what comes across—apart from his courageous skepticism—is the boundless enthusiasm and compassion he has for his subjects. Not only is he not mad at anyone, but he seems positively enthralled by the search for knowledge, the majesty of the universe he is trying to comprehend. It is not hard to see why his book, *Cosmos*, was the best selling science book of all time. Add to that, the fact he was telegenic and charismatic to a remarkable degree, and you have one of the greatest populizers of science of the twentieth century.

Even more impressive, he was among the first to alert the public to the danger of global warming and the potential climatic consequences of the nuclear war: initiating way back in the 1980's a campaign to create an alliance between religion and science to protect the environment. But it is, to me, as a kind of pioneer astronomer—typified by the way he spearheaded SETI, the Search for Extraterrestrial Intelligence— that he is most memorable. His chapter on "Extraterrestrial Intelligence" is perhaps the most wonderful in the entire book. Although he does not spell it out, it is clear that Carl Sagan thinks explorations in religion should be like the search for extraterrestrial intelligence. The full weight of science should be brought to bear on the problem, no matter how intractable. It does not matter that to date there has not been an iota of confirming evidence—not a single instance of an authenticated message from an extraterrestrial to us—brought forth by SETI. What does matter is that the search, and all that it represents to us, goes on undaunted. Worst of all would be to abandon the scientific method and retreat into mysticism.

The range of his mind and his vision is nothing short of breathtaking. His passionate embrace includes the whole of the physical universe, which to Carl Sagan includes the spiritual. By spiritual, he does not mean anything that is not composed of or derived from matter. What he does not embrace, what he unequivocally rejects is an immaterial, transcendental, supernatural world, or manifestation thereof, for which no evidence has been advanced. He would admit that certain conversion experiences, mystical revelations, faith-based intuitions can on occasion be a source or even pipeline to the truth. But only scientific, skeptical openness of mind can determine—if it can ever be determined—whether such insights represent truth or error. In short, you cannot verify faith with faith. Belief in belief is not a means of finding the truth, it is a way of avoiding a painful confrontation with a reality that is considered unbearable.

Not surprisingly, Carl Sagan was fascinated by perhaps the most complex object in the cosmos: the human brain. In *The Dragons of Eden*, in his wonderfully imaginative way, he presents nothing less than a speculative overview of the Darwinian story of evolution. His discussion on the lateralization of the brain— the left and right hemispheric functions—is not only brilliant and clear, but the best I have ever read. Perhaps the only shortcoming in this splendid book is a tendency—in his eagerness to hit a creative home run every time out, and never to settle for a nice single up the middle—to sometimes overreach himself. Example: he suggests that the biological origin of our innate fear of falling might be an ancestral memory of a primeval fear of falling from trees when we were once arboreal creatures. (Nice idea: but what about our far more recent, infantile memories of our fear of falling when we were learning to walk; what about our memories of all the pain that can result from actual falling accidents; or the fact that, of all mammals, our bipedal footing may be the least secure?)

Finally, much as I hold Carl Sagan to be an example of the truly humane skeptic, he fails to realize how rare is that poetic, scientific and spiritual appreciation of the physical universe that he so passionately advocates. He overlooks (as does Richard Dawkins) that even among fellow scientists, there are few who display such a sustained reverence for the wonders of nature (which may be why they are both so very famous: in addition to being world class scientists, they are incomparable, mesmerizing populizers of the beauties of science).

In some ways, of all the scholars and thinkers I have mentioned, Carl Sagan comes closest to our theme. His indomitable search for extraterrestrial intelligence, in the face of the longest of odds, resonates on a very deep level with the human quest to penetrate the mystery of the afterlife. From a psychodynamic standpoint, the continuation of our consciousness or intelligence in the afterlife could represent an extraterrestrial intelligence (in the sense that our surviving after-death consciousness, now no longer earthbound, would be, in whatever form or place it was, literally "extraterrestrial"). So it may be that, unconsciously, the discovery of an actual cosmological, non-fictional E.T.—always a possibility—represents the closest we can presently come to knowing what at least one version of the afterlife might be: an indisputable, not-of-this-world intelligence, the first testimony from another realm, the first proof that there really is "something more" in the universe than just our terrestrial consciousness. And we could always be assured that—no matter how unsettling contact with such an extraterrestrial intelligence might prove to be—we could say: maybe that's what an alien is like, but not us.

This raises the question: If a cosmologist such as Carl Sagan could express such open-minded wonder, perpetual doubt and endless curiosity, why can't a theologian? Why must there be such uniformity, such stasis when it comes to the core tenets of religious doctrine? Why are there no discernible advances, no paradigmatic shifts in two thousand years of theological inquiry? Although it may be of momentous sociological and political import if, for example, the Catholic Church were to revise their ban against abortion or divorce, it would be of no consequence whatever concerning the existence of God and the afterlife. It would have no bearing on the question of the ultimate nature of the world. It is worth noting that most theological change has been of this self-serving reactive sort—to political and sociological pressures that could no longer be safely ignored. The biggest retreat of all has been from the advance of science. Where several hundred years ago, as Carl Sagan pointed out, it was believed the intervention of God was required before a flower could bloom, theology has by now retreated close to fifteen billion years to before the Big Bang!

Which is not, however, how the average person sees it. He or she could not care less about what preceded the Big Bang. It is what comes next after their all-too-brief sojourn on earth is over that worries them. If there is hope after death, it does not matter if there are only molecules, if there is just physics before. In the most important question of all, the average nuts and bolts person is a survival-driven pragmatist. In terms of Maslow's hierarchy of needs, the more the person is endangered, the more the instinct for self preservation will prevail. The more the call is for desperate action, for fight or flight, the greater the need for at least the illusion of certainty. One turns to what has worked best in the past, been most useful, proven most trustworthy. Someone who is faced with the issue of their mortality, who is overwhelmed with the prospect of their extinction, does not have time for the exquisitely patient, self-correcting investigation—that can and often does take centuries—in which science is so adept. When the choice seems only between annihilation or salvation, there will be few who can sustain the quizzical, investigative frame of mind of a Carl Sagan.

Darwin's Belief

In "Why Do We Believe?" Robin Marantz Henig deftly and swiftly reviews the current scientific search for an evolutionary explanation for why belief in God exists. The field is spearheaded by the burgeoning discipline of evolutionary psychology, the latest incarnation of E.O. Wilson's famed 1975 synthesis, *Sociobiology*, which itself was the direct heir of Charles Darwin's epoch-making *The Descent of Man*.

Evolutionary psychology looks for universal human traits that seem necessary for our survival, traits that are likely to have a genetic basis. What is unique about evolutionary psychology is that it does not look for the adaptive value of such traits in the present. It goes back to the original ancestral conditions, when our genome was being formed and—in the context of our lives as hunter-gatherers, and in the ecological conditions that then prevailed—it tries to find the adaptive value *at that time*. As a result, evolutionary psychology has been able to shed light on some seemingly anomalous patterns of behavior: what no longer makes sense or is useful today may very well be the genetic heir of behavior that was once highly adaptive to our ancestors. Adaptive, from the Darwinian standpoint of evolutionary biology, means behavior that contributes to an animal's reproductive fitness—helping it survive, compete, find a mate and, above all, pass its genes into the next generation.

The Darwinian explanation for why belief in God exists, looks for the adaptive benefit that such a belief might have conferred. Did it enhance group fitness by promoting group solidarity (as David Sloan Wilson believes)? Did it supply the emotional glue that made for a tribal spirit, necessary to conduct group hunts and fight off one's enemies? Or was it a mere byproduct—unadaptive in itself—of something entirely different that was adaptive? (This a version of Stephen Jay Gould's and Richard Lewontin's well-known "spandrel" theory, a spandrel being a trait that has no adaptive value of its own, but is an unintended byproduct of something else. "Natural selection made the human brain big," Gould wrote, "but most of our mental properties and potentials may be spandrels—that is, non-adaptive side consequences of building a device with such structural complexity.")

Scott Atran, an anthropologist with a research interest in evolutionary psychology and cognitive science, is a byproduct theorist. As Robin Marantz Henig notes, he sometimes presents his students with a wooden box that he pretends is an African relic. "If you have negative sentiments toward religion," he tells them, "the box will destroy whatever you put inside it." The point of the demonstration is that even students who say they are nonbelievers act as if they believe in something. When he tells them to put their pencil in the box, the nonbelievers do so without hesitation. When he tells them to put their driver's license in, most do, but only after significant hesitation. When he tells them to put their hands in, few comply. Atran wonders, "If they don't believe in God, what exactly are they afraid of?"

Here, I think, is an unintended but compelling example of the difference between a cognitive and a psychodynamic explanation of human behavior. The cognitive explanation will focus naturally on cognitive mechanisms—in this case the unacknowledged, irrational, and vestigial, magical thinking of professed skeptics. But it will focus on primarily one thing—the hidden defect in the supposedly well-functioning, adult, cognitive apparatus. By contrast, a psychodynamic explanation will try to incorporate as many of the relevant dimensions of the human equation, particularly the dynamic unconscious, as it can. These might include, in addition to the cognitive, the emotional, the interpersonal, the irrational, the defensive, the characterological, and the aggressive components in a dynamic interactive pattern meant to be a signature of the individual subject's distinctive personality.

Thus, from a psychodynamic perspective, there could be reasons other than or in addition to cognitive ones for why a presumably rational, adult skeptic might hesitate to put something valuable in the haunted box. First note, that Atran "pretended" that the box was an African relic, thereby admitting a critical deception was a precondition of the success of the experiment. But perhaps this deception was read on some subliminal level by certain perceptive students. If this was some kind of a psychological hoax, if something was up, it is understandable that someone might show, not so much hesitation, as mistrust. Someone might refrain from putting in their hands, not because they feared supernatural vengeance, but because they didn't want to be tricked by a psychologist. Perhaps they were afraid of being mildly shocked, or surprised by something that felt like a creepy dead thing, but was really, say, a ragdog? Maybe, the point of the test was to determine just how mindless and gullible they were and, no matter what they did, they feared, not retribution, but social embarrassment?

Just imagine for a moment you were to participate in Atran's experiment. He shows you a box, tells you it is an African relic, and says, "If you have negative sentiments toward religion, the box will destroy whatever you put inside it." He then instructs you to put in, respectively, your pencil, your wallet, your hands. What would you think? Would you trust him? What is so rational about taking the word of someone who says that to you and then actually doing what he says? It is perhaps more rational, to be immediately on one's guard, to suspect a trick, to incrementally fall prey to a (normal) paranoid frame of mind. Maybe Atran, however, does know what he is talking about, and knows, for example, that reputable African villages have really testified to the damage that has accrued to certain irreligious people who have profanely touched the box. Maybe Atran does not believe this himself, but wants to see if you do. But what if certain people really have been hurt, not because of a curse, but because of an undetected toxic chemical inside the box? Or what if you could not care less about any of the above, but you do care about coming across as insensitively irreligious and you do not want to put your wallet or your hands in the box for the same reason you do not want your family to know that it has been many years since you last went to church?

To make the point even clearer, and to take this out of the laboratory of the research psychologist and into the realm of everyday life, imagine the following. You are about to buy a watch as a birthday present, say, for your father and, while wrapping your gift, the sales clerk, laughing a little self-consciously and perhaps guiltily, says, "It's strange, but the last two people I sold this watch to, died of heart attacks a few weeks later." And almost immediately, recognizing and trying to undo his monumental gaffe, adds, "Of course, that had nothing to do with this. It's a fine watch."

Now, what would you do? Under such a circumstance, is it
really more rational to go ahead and buy the watch from this
particular sales person? A cognitive scientist such as Atran
seems to think so. He makes the assumption that a person
acting rationally will *always refrain* from doing anything that
might be included under the tainted umbrella of superstitious
thinking. But that can be a blinkered viewpoint. There could
be valid, common-sensical reasons for shying away from
violating a religious taboo. Such as for example the pragmatic
desire to save energy. For, anyway you put it, it is a creepy thing
to tell a person out of the blue that there's a curse or a series of
unexplained deaths attached to what looks like a harmless,
everyday object. That's hard to ignore, no matter how
unsuperstitious you are. It is natural to want to think about it.
Just how did this supposed curse or jinx come about? Is there
a simple, understandable explanation? Since you are not a
cognitive scientist investigating the roots of irrational beliefs,
you are not interested—when all you want to do is to buy a
watch or participate in an interesting, but presumably trivial
psychological experiment—in being lured into a weird-
sounding chain of events. What rational reason would an
ordinary person have for doing that?

The cognitive scientist, in order to study a single cognitive
function, will throw out all the other interfering variables. It is
the standard practice of the experimental psychologist who
begins by reducing the unmanagable complexity of life in order
to better understand it. Afterwards, when insight has hopefully
been gained, the new knowledge is brought back and added to
the previous picture and it is presumed that our understanding
has been thereby enriched. But as we have shown, something
funny happens along the way to the artificially reduced,
experimental model in its return trip back to the original, full-

blown, life-style context from which it has been extracted. The cognitive scientist, bewitched by the purity of thought derived from his toy model universe, forgets *to put back all the variables he has originally removed.*

By contrast, the psychodynamic approach aspires to put in as much of the significant human equation—often overlooked by the cognitivist whose principal area of interest is the computer-simulating or computer-like functions of the human mind—as he or she can. The clinical setting used by the psychodynamic psychotherapist will accordingly be deliberately arranged so as to elicit the full subjectivity of the patient, the rich spectrum of whatever he or she has experienced in the past (and if this happens to include having just participated in a psychological experiment, it will focus intensely on all the ways in which *the experimenter, experiment and subject were dynamically, consciously and unconsciously perceived and intertwined.*

Pascal Boyer, an anthropologist and psychologist, is another leading byproduct theorist closer to our theme. Religious beliefs, he says, are "minimally counterintuitive." They are weird enough to capture your attention and stick in your mind but not so weird that you reject out of hand. "A tree that talks is minimally counterintuitive, and you might believe it as a supernatural agent. A tree that talks and flies and time travels is maximally counterintuitive and you are more likely to reject it." It is immediately apparent that a God who has a human personality but who is infinitely more intelligent than you, or a God who decides to visit the earth in the shape of a man, is minimally counterintuitive.

And here we have a wonderfully simple cognitive explanation for why it is so nearly impossible to conceive of a complex relationship with God. An in-depth relationship with a real God, and all that it would entail, is *a maximally counterintuitive idea*. But a God who is ever vigilant, protective and watches over us, who can evoke and magically gratify the deepest wishes of our infancy and childhood, especially when we are most in need, is a very different story. It is a belief system with a narrative arc as hard to resist as it is easy to understand.

In a recent book, *Primates and Philosophers*, the renowned primatologist Frans de Waal argues that the roots of morality can be seen in the social behavior of monkeys and apes. Currently the director of the Living Links Center at Emory University, he has spent years observing nonhuman primates. He is convinced that, "Morality is as firmly grounded in neurobiology as anything else we do or are." The roots of empathy can clearly be seen in certain behaviors of chimpanzees, such as mutual grooming. He has seen, for example, on occasion, an adult chimpanzee helping a frightened young chimp down from a tree. Rescue-minded chimpanzees, who cannot swim, have drowned in zoo moats trying to save others. Rhesus monkeys, who can get food by pulling a chain that would also deliver an electric shock to a companion, will sometimes starve themselves for days.

Looking back, we can easily imagine Darwin cheering on the researches of evolutionary biologists like Frans de Waal. As Janet Brown so brilliantly shows in her book, *Darwin's Origin of Species*, the founder of evolutionary biology anticipated many of the questions and conflicts facing evolutionists today. She is right to point out that contemporary intelligent design (ID) theorists are at bottom a modern variant of William Paley's classic watchmaker argument, the argument that *The Origin of Species* effectively demolished. From that standpoint, the biochemist Michael Bethe's claim that the design of the protein is too complicated to have arisen by natural selection without the help of an intelligent designer is little better than disguised creation science. It's no more probable, for example, than the young earth creationist's claim that all the fossils ever found were laid down at the time of Noah's flood. (Only creationists, she points out, insist on taking everything in the Bible to be literally true.)

One of the greatest of living Darwin scholars, Janet Brown, shows how deeply colored by emotion every competing (so-called scientific) theory of evolution since Darwin has been. Darwin himself, as is well known, was tormented by fears that he would be ostracized by his fellow Victorians. That was hardly the case, but it is a sobering thought. If even the greatest evolutionist was so susceptible to being influenced by his emotions on the key issues, we can imagine how difficult the analogous conflict is for the ordinary person.

The psychodynamic perspective on the roots of religious belief does not contradict the cognitive, neurobiological or evolutionary viewpoint. It merely adds the much neglected basic emotions. It incorporates, in a way that cognitive science and evolutionary psychology do not, the dynamic unconscious. In addition to the researcher's laboratory, the field biologist's free-roaming animals, it brings in the clinician's office. Most significantly, it strives to capture the unpredictable complexity of a lived life. It does not try, as does the cognitivist, to assemble a whole person essentially from the problem-solving functions of the brain. It does not try to leapfrog from the evolutionary traits we share with our non-human primate cousins straight to the fuzzy beginnings of an emergent human self. Instead, it embraces a more holistic, hierarchical and layered picture of a dynamically interacting, often conflicted, never simply mechanistic, and always unique person.

Lonely Hearts Of The Cosmos

Such was the marvelous phrase with which Dennis Overbye once summed up the Homeric odyssey of the contemporary cosmologist. One such lonely heart is Alan Guth. *The Inflationary Universe* is his own, wonderfully personalized account of how he happened to come up with what many consider the reigning cosmological paradigm in the world today. His central idea is that immediately after the big bang, an inflation began, moving with the speed of light, taking place in less than a second, and unimaginably expanding the infant universe to much of its current size. Driving this incredible expansion is what Guth called inflationary energy, and creating the inflationary energy was the repulsive effect of what Guth hypothesized to be an intrinsically unstable false vacuum.

More than any of his predecessors, Guth speculated on what might have happened *before* the big bang. The theory he eventually comes up with postulates that random quantum fluctuations, based on the rules of quantum mechanics, can regularly—through the repulsive effect of a false vacuum—produce the explosive force necessary for a big bang to occur. The staggering implication is there were a huge number of pocket universes, of which our present universe is just one, that existed *prior* to the big bang. Furthermore, it is theoretically possible, says Guth, in principle—for an advanced civilization—to one day create "a laboratory universe." Alan Guth himself calls the inflationary universe a "theory of how all the matter in our universe came to be," and because he thinks what happened before can happen again, he is a believer in an eternal inflationary universe.

Is it possible there could be proof for such a far-ranging, incredible theory? Well, in 1992, in an historic meeting, the results of the Cosmic Background Explorer satellite, known as COBE, were announced. One of the three instruments aboard the satellite, the Differential Microwave Radiometer (DMR) was dedicated to measuring the nonuniformities in the temperature of the background cosmic radiation. Since Alan Guth's original inflationary theory well over ten years previously had made precise predictions as to what these hypothesized nonuniformities in the temperature of the background cosmic radiation were, here was a golden opportunity for possible experimental verification. And what did the COBE results show? That the agreement between the data and the predictions of inflation were nearly perfect! As Alan Guth would later reflect on the greatest moment of his cosmologist's life, "To a theoretical physicist, there is no greater joy than to see that this curious activity that we call calculation—the depositing of ink on paper . . . —can actually tell us something about entity!"

In 1980, Paul J. Steinhardt, a brilliant young particle physicist, attended a seminar by the then unknown Alan Guth, who was in the process of unveiling to the world his startling, new inflationary model of the universe. Astute enough to know a paradigm shift when he saw one, Paul Steinhardt more or less became a cosmologist on the spot. His recent book, *Endless Universe—Beyond the Big Bang*, written with his collaborator and co-discoverer, Neil Turok, is the story of the revolutionary new model of the universe they themselves would eventually create. For a non-physicist such as myself, the book was a pleasure to read. Wonderfully imaginative and fearlessly creative, it captures the passion and the joy that drives and sustains the solitary pioneer theoretician.

Their final theory, called the cyclic model, is nothing less than a bold challenge to the accepted picture of the big bang, and to the future of the universe. It is an alternative to the standard inflationary universe. It postulates not one, but an endless series of big bangs. It asserts the universe is basically the same everywhere, both before and after the big bang. There is no multiverse. No pocket universe. No empty spaces and no infinite expansion.

Amazingly, the cyclic model agrees with everything Alan Guth's inflationary model says about the universe, from about one second after the big bang occurred until now. There could not be a greater disagreement, however, about what occurred immediately after the big bang, the critical time, according to Alan Guth, in which the universe was supposed to exponentially inflate. The cyclic model denies any such inflation ever took place!

Then what drove the undeniable expansion of the early universe? Dark energy, not inflationary energy, according to Steinhardt and Turok. Their new theory borrows heavily from string theory, especially its latest incarnation as Matrix Theory. Single-handedly conceived by Ed Witten, the world's greatest string theorist, Matrix Theory revolutionized physics by replacing vibrating strings—as the fundamental building blocks of the subatomic world—with new objects called *branes* (short for "membranes"). The new objects entailed adding yet another hidden dimension to the universe, one whose job it was to keep the branes separated.

Steinhardt and Turok's big idea was to wonder what would happen if two branes randomly collided? And what might cause such a random collision? Their answer was to nominate the newly discovered concept of dark (because invisible) energy. The result? In a moment of inspiration, arrived at together, they realized: *two branes colliding could, under the right conditions, produce a big bang!* The idea if true would revolutionize cosmology. It would mean, in contrast to Alan Guth, that time and space and matter did not originate in a single big bang. It would mean that something did not come out of nothing; that our universe was not created by "quantum fluctuation, quantum tunneling, quantum jitters." That the big bang was not a one-time occurrence. That before our world there was a brane world out of which our universe emerged. That such worlds are periodically drawn together and collide at regular intervals of about a trillion years.

Is it possible now there could be proof for this even more fantastic-sounding cyclic model? Well, in 2003 a meeting was called to announce the results of the mission called WMAP (the follow-up to the pioneering 1989 NASA satellite called COBE). Astonishingly, the results not only confirmed the 1980 predictions made by Alan Guth's inflationary model, but also the new predictions of the competing cyclic model! Not surprisingly, an overjoyed Paul Steinhardt and Neil Turok conclude their mind-boggling book with an exuberant challenge: "Let the debate begin!"

As much as I loved *Endless Universe: Beyond the Big Bang*, I would like to give voice to a nagging philosophical caveat. There is a difference between a prediction and a postdiction. The remarkable predictions made by Alan Guth's inflationary model—electrifyingly confirmed by COBE in 1992 and by WMAP in 2003—were made in 1980 (and refined thereafter). The postdictions made by Steinhardt and Turok were all made in the twenty-first century, over twenty years after the birth of the inflationary model. To their everlasting credit, however, Steinhardt and Turok have gone well out on the limb and made precise *predictions* that, if confirmed in the future, would decisively dislodge the inflationary picture as the reigning cosmological paradigm and experimentally confirm the dazzling new cyclic model. As they truly say at the book's end, these are exciting times for cosmology.

Regardless of the outcome, there is a lesson for you and me and for all of us here. As they repeatedly make crystal clear in both their books, what drives Alan Guth, David Steinhardt and Neil Turok, despite their manifest technical brilliance, is an insatiable, child-like but fearless curiosity in the face of the biggest questions of all. Where did we come from? Where are we going? What made us, or who made us? Does there seem to be any plan, design or purpose to the cosmos? What is the relationship of the universe to us? Is there any relationship between the big bang and the origin of life as we know it?

You will say, perhaps, yes, but they are scientists, not theologians, and of course that is true. But the real difference, I would suggest, is not so much defined by the questions they ask, but by their method of inquiry. Each of these pioneer cosmologists has not only invested their lives and the fortunes of their families on the daring theories they have proposed, but they have bent over backwards to submit their ideas to the most excruciating, rigorous, experimental tests that modern science can devise. Each of them is prepared to give up their lifelong dream if a single initial experiment refutes it!

By comparison, the contemporary theologian cannot be refuted, because he or she does not submit their belief to an independent standard of validation. They may be wrong but they cannot find that out if at all until after they die. Typically, the model of the cosmos they endorse—essentially based on the hypothetical Supreme Being who created the big bang 14 to 15 billion years ago and who watches over us and will reveal Himself and meet us after we die—was passed on to them when they were very small children. It is a picture of the cosmos that not only cannot by definition be refuted, but which demands unquestioning allegiance, and which will punish unbelievers with an eternal retribution.

Is it any surprise when we look back over two thousand years of passionate theological inquiry, by admittedly some brilliant minds—and look for the analogous paradigm shift—we find none? That is unless you are prepared to consider that the admission that the six days Genesis says it took God to create heaven and earth was only a metaphor—and that the Bible cannot be read in its entirety as literally true—counts as a paradigm shift.

Nor does this mean there have not been courageous religious thinkers who have profoundly wrestled with these same, unanswerable questions. Just that when you eliminate the option to register and explore to one's heart's content any and every doubt, you simultaneously close the door on the freedom that is required to think creatively.

CHAPTER SEVEN

THE THEOLOGY OF THE UNCONSCIOUS

Several years ago, I received a mysterious, anonymous letter, requesting me to send copies of the same letter to at least two other people. If I did so, I might enjoy the same good fortune that had been known to befall several people who were willing to comply. Were I to disregard the letter, however, I might incur the same bad luck reported by at least three others.

The letter had an immediate, jarring effect. It was a chain letter operating on the carrot and stick principle. Do what I say and you get something wonderful. Don't do what I say, and just wait and see what happens. The choices offered me could not be simpler. Either pass the chain letter along or throw it in the waste basket and take your chances. Since I knew at once I was not going to send such a letter to another person—that would be unethical—it meant throwing the letter away.

Yet, much to my chagrin and embarrassment, I found that surprisingly hard to do. What if there was something to the letter? Could I be absolutely certain that nothing sinister would befall me if I decided to break the chain? Why had the sender refused to sign their name, unless they had something to hide? Was it possible the sender was someone who knew me?

My instinct, the healthy part of my mind, said don't be silly, throw the letter away, but something stopped me. Instead, putting the letter to the side, I tried not to think about it. A day passed, another day. The more I tried not to think about it, the more I thought about it. There was only one way to end my conflict. Screwing up my courage, I broke the chain and threw the letter away.

Like Atran's African relic, the letter put me in touch with the irrational part of my mind. There was nothing about the letter that made sense, nothing that could make me respect it, yet its power to cast some kind of temporary superstitious spell over me was undeniable. It did that by reaching down, by appealing solely to an early primitive part of my personality.

This book has been an attempt to answer the question with which it began: Why in over thirty years of private practice, after listening to hundreds and hundreds of patients' dreams, had I not once encountered the presence of God, the appearance of an angel, or heard heaven mentioned? It was remarkable to me, and continues to be remarkable, how otherwise sensitive, thoughtful, inquisitive, sometimes brilliant patients could suddenly turn mute when the subject of the afterlife came up. As though they had given no real thought, unless it smacked them in the face, to the fact of their own death. Was it possible they could be interested in everything under the sun but had no curiosity about one of the greatest questions of all time— what happens to their consciousness after they die? Or, as I began to suspect—because of the unconscious denial of death and the existential dread of thinking about one's own nonexistence—had their natural curiosity switched off at a very early age?

In the book, I rely on the psychodynamic psychotherapeutic approach which in turn advocates the introduction—between the contemporary biologist's neurotransmitters, the social scientist's statistics and the cognitivist's cognitive mechanisms—the impact of the dynamic unconscious. Once we do that, a lot of the mystery evaporates. Although we like to talk about God as something incomprehensible, something inexpressible, we forget that our very first experience is with the unknowable. We begin our lives as pre-verbal, existential beings who immediately enter into a symbiotic relationship with a seemingly magical, omnipotent caretaker who knows our every need. Is it any wonder, imprinted in our unconscious, is a deep, lifelong yearning for a cosmic parent to be called upon primarily when we are most in need? As I have tried to show, this cosmic, parental figure is both masculine and feminine. Masculine when protection or vengeance is called for. Feminine when we want a God-like being to take pity on us and intervene because she loves us. It is neither all-powerful, all-knowing, nor all-good. It is not a cohesive, but a transient being, that comes and goes, to be used selectively on a crisis-intervention basis.

Not surprisingly, since the psychodynamic approach is a bottom-up perspective, the picture it reveals is characterized by inconsistency, self-contradiction and instability. It barely resembles the parables and narratives of organized religion. There is, however, as I have said, a genuine yearning for a transcendental "something," a residue of childish hunger for a cosmic and personal connection that we never entirely surmount.

What I Believe

I'll close with a final thought experiment. Imagine what has always seemed impossible, actually occurs: *science proves that God exists!* With, of course, a big assist from God who, as even Richard Dawkins noted in *The God Delusion*, "could easily reveal himself" if he chose. And how might he reveal Himself? Well, the philosopher Bertrand Russell once said that—were he one day to see all the events of tomorrow clearly and accurately written across the sky, he would then believe in the existence of God. But there could be other ways. God might return to earth, in whatever shape He wanted to, and just keep performing one miracle after another, until even the most diehard atheist would have to cry uncle. Once we make the assumption that God has chosen to reveal Himself, we see how easy it would be. There would, of course, always be the chance that the God who was revealing Himself was not the God we have always believed in, the God of the Bible, but a trickster God. Or not a God at all, but a superhumanly intelligent and unimaginably scientifically advanced extraterrestrial who, for one reason or another, was interested in duping us, but few would take such doubts seriously.

Now what would the impact be on science as a body of knowledge, in particular on professional skeptics such as Carl Sagan (supposing he were still alive) and Richard Dawkins, who have banked their careers on the opposite result? As for science, the proof of the existence of God would not only constitute by far the greatest scientific discovery in history, but it would necessitate at the very least a revolution in the structure of physics. To the four fundamental forces—electromagnetism, gravity, the strong and the weak nuclear force—the supernatural power of God would have to be added. For who could now deny that miracles—in the strict scientific sense of immaterial, invisible, supernatural forces being able to interact with wholly physical objects—really do occur?

It would, however, be a somewhat different story for someone such as Carl Sagan and Richard Dawkins. I would guess at first they would have to be more than a little embarrassed. But the core of skepticism is fearlessness in the face of even the most unpleasant of truths, so I see them rallying quickly, climbing on the bandwagon and eager to be on the cutting edge of a glorious new scientific frontier—the race to understand how God created the universe.

Now what about the reverse—*science disproves the existence of God?* Although traditionally religion has long counted on the impossibility of this ever coming to pass, it is far easier to imagine than the opposite. Think of science advancing to such a mind-boggling state that it can (as per Alan Guth) create universes in a laboratory, engineer life in its full complexity at will, explain in a thoroughly naturalistic way exactly how the big bang happened. Or imagine biblical scholarship, so fantastically developed that it can go back in time and piece together thousands of historical facts that unanimously and conclusively demonstrate that authorship of the Bible was wholly and only human?

In the advent of such an admittedly astounding occurrence, it would require no leap of the imagination to see that the foundation of theology would be demolished and that the belief system of the devoutly religious would be dealt at the very least a crippling blow. It is one thing to say, as the skeptic does, "I prefer to live in a world ruled by reason and humanism." It is another to say, as the believer does, "I cannot imagine and would not want to live in a world without God. Such a world would be without meaning." But what if life is without meaning in the cosmological sense, what if life arose accidentally, as many leading scientists believe, a random if incredible, statistical fluke?

Saying this, I am aware in this thought experiment, that the skeptic has far less to lose than the believer. The skeptic after all loses only a single important belief. The believer, however, has lost just about everything that matters in the world. My point is just that, although everyone ultimately must choose their own cosmology, hopefully that choice won't be based on fear, magical thinking or child-life neediness.

If the practice of psychotherapy teaches anything, it shows that life is a never-ending struggle of encounters with unimaginable and unacceptable realities. No one, for example, thinks they or anyone they love are going to die, but everyone does. No one can imagine what it can be like not to exist, and yet everyone—in the sense of one day having to give up everything about their life on earth which they treasured—will meet that fate. Nor is this particularly mysterious. We are programmed by evolution to be born, to live, to suffer deeply, to celebrate when we can, to endure random tragedy and to die. And like it or not, we all find that somehow we are able, however imperfectly and resentfully, to do this.

The unfortunate clash between science and religion is not one between reason and emotion. The skeptic is not or does not have to be, as many believe, cold-hearted and mean-spirited. At his best, as in the case of Carl Sagan, he has passion and wonder, as well as reason and doubt.

As a therapist—if you look in the eyes of someone who is talking about the afterlife—you often can see a childlike self. You see a core of wonder we all start out with, but which somehow has ceased to grow. Both culture at large and religion are complicitous, both have tried to manipulate and micromanage that innate cosmic curiosity. But no one, no authority can tell you what your life means to you or should mean to you. Science or theology can tell you what they think their answer is to what exists out there, what lies in store for us, and what came before us, but they cannot tell you what that answer means to you. An individual's truth can only be individually interpreted. You can hand that over to an authority, but you are still making an interpretation: to attain truth is to identify with someone who represents it.

Having said that, it is obvious that my own belief system does not matter, or should only matter to me. But if I were asked, I would say I personally believe:

That the Bible is a great but flawed book, best understood in the context of the times in which it was written; a repository of wondrous poetry and timeless folk wisdom, but not an infallible guide on how to live one's life in the modern world; not a blueprint of how heaven and earth were created, not a picture of the afterlife. That the cosmologists are the true theologians of today, the ones most likely to take us closer to the mystery of how our universe was created. That the meaning of our lives is not measured by whether the cosmos is indifferent to our suffering or not, but depends far more on what we make of our relationship to the world in which we find ourselves. That the best answer to the meaningfulness of our death or the question of the afterlife will be found in the life that preceded it. That as a nation, far more than scientific illiteracy, we suffer from what could be called *existential illiteracy*: the failure to wonder in an intelligent, creative and mature way about the greatest question of all—the puzzle of our own existence.

As I write this, there is a report on the science channel on the latest findings of SETI, which always seems to be the same. Decades of the most diligent, ultra-high tech, astronomical scanning of the skies have yet to produce a single authenticated instance of a message being received from an extraterrestrial intelligence. Undaunted, they continue to search. Some of the best minds in the world are devoting their lives to finding in the vastness of the cosmos a possible clue to the riddle of our existence, the mystery of life. Whatever the answer may be, whether it be joyful and uplifting or dispiriting, frightening and isolating, they are more than ready to accept it, to deal with it, to discover whatever meaning there may be.

I, for one, find that comforting.

REFERENCES

Alper, G. (1992) *Portrait of the Artist as a Young Patient.* New York: Insight books/Plenum Publishing.
(2003) *Knowing If It's The Real Thing.* New York: Taylor Trade Publishing.
(2003) *Self-Defense In A Narcissistic World.* New York: Hamilton Books, an imprint of University Press of America.

Barrett, W. (1979) *The Illusion Of Technique.* New York: Doubleday.

Bateson, G. (1972) *Steps To An Ecology Of The Mind.* New York: Random House.

Bollas, C. (1987) "The Transformational Object" in *The Shadow Of The Object.* New York: Columbia University Press.

Brown, J. (2006) *Darwin's Origin of Species.* New York: Grove/Atlantic, Inc.

Darwin, C. (1958) *The Origin of Species.* New York: The New American Library of World Literature (originally published 1859).
(1981) *The Descent Of Man.* Princeton, New Jersey: Princeton University Press.

Dawkins, R. (2003) *A Devil's Chaplain.* New York: Houghton Mifflin Co.
(2006) *The God Delusion.* New York: Houghton Mifflin Co.

Dennett, D.C. (2006) *Breaking The Spell.* London: Viking

De Waal, F. (2006) *Primates and Philosophers*. Princeton, New Jersey: Princeton University Press.

Dostoyevsky, F. (1968) *Notes From The Underground* (1864) in *Great Short Works of Fyodor Dostoyevsky*, Introduction by Ronald Hingley. New York: Harper and Row Publishers. (1968) *The Gambler* in *Great Short Works of Fyodor Dostoyevsky*, Introduction by Ronald Hingley. New York: Harper and Row Publishers.

Frank, J. (1995) *Dostoyevsky: The Miraculous Years*. Princeton, New Jersey: Princeton University Press.

Freud, S. (1927) *The Future Of An Illusion*. New York: Doubleday & Co. Inc.

Gould, S.J. (1989) *Wonderful Life*. New York: W.W. Norton & Co.

(2002) *The Structure of Evolutionary Theory*. Cambridge, Mass.: The Belknap Press of Harvard University Press.

Guth, A. (1997) *The Inflationary Universe*. Cambridge, Mass.: Perseus Books.

Hamilton, W.D. (1996) *Narrow Roads of Gene Land*. New York: W.H. Freeman and Co.

Hammer, D. (2004) *The God Gene*. New York: Knopf Publishing.

Harris, S. (2004) *The End of Faith*. New York: W.W. Norton and Co.

Henig, R.M. (2007) "Why Do We Believe?" in March 4, 2007 *New York Times Magazine*.

James, W. (1981) *The Principles of Psychology*. Cambridge, Mass.: Harvard University Press (1981). (1999) *The Varieties of Religious Experience*. New York: Random House (first published 1902).

Jung, C. (1958) *Answer To Job*. Princeton, New Jersey: Princeton University Press.

Kübler-Ross, E. (1969) *On Death And Dying.* New York: Scribner Publishing.

Kushner, H. (2004) *When Bad Things Happen To Good People.* New York: Random House (originally published 1981).

Lorenz, K. (1981) *The Foundations Of Ethology.* New York: Simon and Schuster.

Maslow, A. (1954) *Motivation And Personality.* New York: Harper, 1954.

Nuland, S. (1993) *How We Die.* New York: Knopf.

Overbye, D. (1990) *Lonely Hearts of the Cosmos.* New York: Backbay Books

PDM Task Force (2006) *Psychodynamic Diagnostic Manual.* Silver Spring, MD: Alliance of Psychoanalytic Organizations.

Ramachandran, V.S., and Blakeslee, S. (1998) *Phantoms in the Brain.* New York: HarperCollins Publisher.

Roach, M. (2005) *Spook Science Tackles The Afterlife.* New York: W.W. Norton.

Sacks, O. (2007) "A Neurologist's Notebook: A Bolt From The Blue." *The New Yorker* (7/23/2007).

Sagan, C. (1977) *The Dragons Of Eden.* New York: Random House Publishing Group.

(2006) *The Varieties of Scientific Experience: A Personal View of the Search for God.* New York: Penguin Press.

Steinhardt, P. (2007) and Turok, N. *Endless Universe.* New York: Doubleday.

Stenger, V. (2007) *God: The Failed Hypothesis.* Amherst, New York: Prometheus Publishing.

Warren, R. (2007) *The Purpose Driven Life.* New York: Zondervan Publishing.

Weinberg, S. (1997) *The First Three Minutes.* New York: Basic Books.

(2001) *Facing Up*. Cambridge, Mass.: Harvard University Press.

Wilson, D.S. (2007) *Evolution For Everyone*. New York: Delacorte Press.

Wilson, E.O. (1994) *The Naturalist*. New York: Warner Books.

For sales, editorial information, subsidiary rights information
or a catalog, please write or phone or e-mail

iBooks
Manhanset House
Shelter Island Hts., NY 11965-0342, US
Sales: 1-800-68-BRICK
Tel: 212-427-7139
www.ibooksinc.com
bricktower@aol.com

www.Ingram.com

For sales in the UK and Europe please contact our distributor,
Gazelle Book Services
White Cross Mills
Lancaster, LA1 4XS, UK
Tel: (01524) 68765 Fax: (01524) 63232
email: jacky@gazellebooks.co.uk